MW00814906

To: Sister Donna G Shive
The Lord Bless You & Keep You fit
for His Service!!

4-29-2017.

The Christian in
CONTEMPORARY
Nigerian Society

Musa Adziba Mambula

WESTBOW
PRESS®
A DIVISION OF THOMAS NELSON
& ZONDERVAN

Copyright © 2016 Musa Adziba Mambula.

All rights reserved. No part of this book may be used or reproduced by any means, graphic, electronic, or mechanical, including photocopying, recording, taping or by any information storage retrieval system without the written permission of the author except in the case of brief quotations embodied in critical articles and reviews.

All Scripture quotations, unless otherwise indicated, are taken from the Holy Bible, New International Version®, NIV®. Copyright ©1973, 1978, 1984, 2011 by Biblica, Inc.™ Used by permission of Zondervan. All rights reserved worldwide. www.zondervan.com The "NIV" and "New International Version" are trademarks registered in the United States Patent and Trademark Office by Biblica, Inc.™

Scripture quotations marked (TLB) are taken from The Living Bible copyright © 1971. Used by permission of Tyndale House Publishers, Inc., Carol Stream, Illinois 60188. All rights reserved.

This book is a work of non-fiction. Unless otherwise noted, the author and the publisher make no explicit guarantees as to the accuracy of the information contained in this book and in some cases, names of people and places have been altered to protect their privacy.

WestBow Press books may be ordered through booksellers or by contacting:

WestBow Press
A Division of Thomas Nelson & Zondervan
1663 Liberty Drive
Bloomington, IN 47403
www.westbowpress.com
1 (866) 928-1240

Because of the dynamic nature of the Internet, any web addresses or links contained in this book may have changed since publication and may no longer be valid. The views expressed in this work are solely those of the author and do not necessarily reflect the views of the publisher, and the publisher hereby disclaims any responsibility for them.

Any people depicted in stock imagery provided by Thinkstock are models, and such images are being used for illustrative purposes only. Certain stock imagery © Thinkstock.

ISBN: 978-1-5127-6469-7 (sc)
ISBN: 978-1-5127-6468-0 (e)

Library of Congress Control Number: 2016919138

Print information available on the last page.

WestBow Press rev. date: 12/21/2016

DEDICATION

To all brothers and sisters in contemporary societies across the globe who are persecuted for their faith in Jesus Christ as their Lord and Savior.

PREFACE

Christians in the 21ˢᵗ century Nigerian society are faced with overwhelming arrays of threats, intimidation, harassment, difficult circumstances, and senseless killings, abductions and terrorism which have displaced over one million Christians since 2009 in Northeastern Nigeria. Christians in Nigeria strongly believe that the Bible is a Sacred Scripture, the Living and written Words of God that give them the faith and resilience to trust God more and more everyday as they face persecution day after day. They know and understand that the pages of the Bible are filled with both the languages of peace and violence. In this sense and respect, the Bible as a sacred book is absolutely at home in the Christian home, family church, and the contemporary society. In as much as the Christians have advocated for peace and forgiveness over the years, they are also caught up between the so-called Islamic Jihads and their individual inward spiritual struggles with a theology of violence and peace. Christianity and Islam in pluralistic Nigerian society have the greatest number of adherence in the most populous black nation in the world. Christians are faced with tremendous challenges of being involved at large as their responsibility to faithfully serve God, church, family, and their community. Their relationship must be built upon their Christian values, moral foundation of Biblical understanding, knowledge, beliefs, faith, and their day to day Christian testimony and lifestyle. As a historic "peace church", the church of the brethren in Nigeria has a responsibility to help change the language of violence and the Nigerian nation in presenting peaceful resolutions to conflicts and violence weather in the home, within the community, to the internally displaced persons, or nationally. The in her struggle must fight corruption, discrimination and injustice, ethnicity, religious bigotry and denominationalism through Interfaith programs, Christian -Muslim Mutual Relationships, Workshops, Seminars and conferences, and dialogue. There must be a show of respect and tolerance for different cultures, languages, beliefs and integrity. The physical health of individuals, families, and communities are necessary for our growth, unity, and development. Christians must be prepared to face the challenges in contemporary Nigerian society with resilience and determination.

ACKNOWLEDGEMENT

While writing this book, I have been encouraged by my dear wife Sarah "Digni"(sweeter than honey), to whom I owe much and the extraordinary contributions and support of my children- Christopher and wife Grace, Beatrice and husband Pelte, Ruth and husband Alfred, and Anna Mambula.

I also wish to acknowledge profoundly from my heart the tremendous support, love, care, and every progress facilitated by Mary Ann Moyer Kulp who retyped the entire manuscripts, edited, made suggestions and wrote the introduction/overview. To my daughter Beatrice J. Dangombe, in spite of her very busy schedule volunteered to put in some finishing touches to the final work.

May God's blessings, and anointing be on all who have directly or indirectly contributed in one way or the other to the success of this publication.

With regards to quotations, and illustration credits and some materials used in the Timeline and some graphic pictures, I acknowledge everyone including the media for permission to quote from their materials or sources. I have endeavored to obtain permission to reprint if copyright was involved. In few cases however, where I did not succeed in my attempts to contact a copyright holder, I hope in such instances that my intention would be taken in good spirit.

Ultimately, my greatest gratitude goes to my Lord and Savior

Jesus Christ the Son of the Living God who died and set me free from sin and made me a join heir of His Kingdom.

I have been encouraged through the words of Apostle Paul from 2 Corinthians 1:8-11 (The New Jerusalem Bible) "So in the hardships we underwent in Asia, we want you to be quite certain, brothers, that we were under extraordinary pressure, beyond our powers of endurance, so that we gave up all hope even of surviving. In fact, we were carrying the sentence of death within our own selves, so that we should be forced to trust not in ourselves but in God, who raises the dead. He did save us from such a death and will save us—we are relying on Him to do so. Your prayer for us will contribute to this, so that, for God's favor shown to us as the result of the prayers of so many, thanks too may be given by many on our behalf.

CONTENTS

INTRODUCTION/OVERVIEW

In the 21st century, Christians in Nigeria are faced with an overwhelming array of challenges in all walks of life. The purpose of this book is to consider these challenges and to suggest means of meeting them. Christians especially are charged with living in such a manner as to contribute to the health and strength of their society.

But even prior to the Christian's involvement in society at large is his responsibility to his God and his family. Family relationships must be built upon the moral foundation of Biblical knowledge and belief. Thus, underpinning the Christian's lifestyle and actions is the Bible and all of its teachings; every action should be based upon scriptural precepts.

To a large extent, the family depends upon the Church and its ministry for guidance and support in creating a healthy and moral atmosphere in the home. Thus, the theological training of pastors plays a significant role in society. Together, families and pastors, leaders from every facet of life, will be joined together in the mission to create a healthy society.

The challenges in this mission center upon identifying the problems and their make-up, and planning strategies for dealing with them. This book will undertake to examine a few of the most pressing issues:

The first is religious violence in Nigeria, with emphasis on conflict resolution. As one of the historic "peace churches," the Church of the Brethren (EYN) has a responsibility to lead the nation in presenting peaceful resolutions to all forms of violence, whether in the home, the community, or nationally. The issue of religious violence is particularly pressing because of recent activities of the terrorist group, Boko Haram in the North.

Following closely on the issue of violence is that of corruption at all levels, from personal to political. Until corruption and immoral behavior are ended, members and institutions of society cannot thrive.

The third problem to be discussed is, unfortunately, frequently linked with corruption: the field of politics, office-seeking, and elections. The Christian bears a huge responsibility in this area, to take an active part in educating himself and the general public regarding the issues impacted by the election, and to use his vote in support of candidates who best represent healthy interests of the community and nation.

Finally, the physical health of the individual and community is of vital interest to all. In recent years, the most pressing health crisis has been that of HIV/AIDS. The community is a victim of this disease as well as the gatekeeper in the sense that it holds the answers to prevention, treatment, and eventual eradication. The issues of prevention, treatment, and counseling are all part of the approach which the community and nation must take to respond to this most grievous of all the challenges to the health of the Nigerian nation.

As we consider the role of the Christian ip-n contemporary Nigerian society, we will examine the various ways in which he is affected by its challenges and his responsibility in meeting them and contributing to solutions. The Christian is not alone; he is but one part in the overall picture of a nation struggling to take its place in the 21st century world.

CHAPTER ONE

The Christian and the Bible in Contemporary Nigeria

To examine the role of the Christian in society, it is important to clarify the meaning of the word "Christian." I am a Christian--perhaps you are, too. But what does that mean exactly? It is true that many people are born from Christian homes, have Christian names, are baptized in the name of God the Father, Jesus Christ the Son, and the Holy Spirit, participate in and partake of the Holy Communion as required by church rules and regulations, attend Sunday worship services and fellowships including Sunday School class and Bible Studies. But the simple question is, do these things make one a Christian? Are you a Christian? If so, how do you know that you are?

To be a Christian, you must first believe that Jesus Christ is the Son of God. That in itself is no small matter. But if it is true that you believe this, if it is true that you are a Christian, it changes everything, because if the Christ you believe in is God, then all that He said and did is deeply significant. It influences the way you see, take and use the Word of God, which is the Bible, in living your life in a contemporary society like Nigeria.

Who is a Christian? Pickering (1972) explains the marks of a Christian:

- ➤ A Christian is a person who has been born again. (1 Peter 1:23, John 3:3)
- ➤ A Christian is a person who does not seek salvation through works. (Eph. 2:9, Rom. 4:6)
- ➤ A Christian is a person who shows by his works that he has been given salvation through Christ. (Titus 2:13-14)
- ➤ A Christian is a person who builds on the sure foundation. (1 Cor. 3:11)
- ➤ A Christian is a person who confesses Christ to his fellows. (Rom. 10:10)
- ➤ A Christian is a person who serves the Lord Jesus Christ and waits for his coming. (1Thess. 1:9-10)
- ➤ A Christian is a person who carries the message of salvation to others, beseeching men, saying, "We implore you on Christ's behalf: Be reconciled to God." (2 Cor. 5:20)
- ➤ A Christian is a person who abounds in faith. (Acts 6:5; 2 Cor.5:20)
- ➤ A Christian is a person who continues and is strong in faith. (Acts14:22, Rom. 4:20)
- ➤ A Christian is a person who stands fast in faith. (1 Cor. 16:13)

Now that we have seen precisely who a Christian is, let us consider what the Bible is and what it means to the Christian and how it helps him live in contemporary Nigerian society. The Holy Bible, simply explained, is the Word of God written through divine inspiration. The book of Timothy (3:16) clearly states: "All Scripture is God--breathed and is useful for teaching, rebuking, correcting, and training in righteousness." In First Thessalonians 2:13 we read these words: "And we also thank God continually when we received the Word of God which you heard from us, you accepted it not as

2

human word, but as actually the Word of God which is indeed at work in you who believe." And in Hebrews 1:1, God's final word: His Son says, "In the past God spoke to our ancestors through the prophets at many times in various ways." Finally, in Second Peter 1:21: "For prophecy never had its origin in the human will, but prophets, though human, spoke from God as they were carried along by the Holy Spirit."

The Bible, God's Word, is also like a light that shines on our path to help us stay on track and avoid the pitfalls in our faith pilgrimage, as expressed in Matthew 7:14 and Psalms 119:105. Phillips (2007) said that every Christian alive today is a work in progress. "For it is God who works in you to will and to act in order to fulfill His good purpose." (Phil. 2:13)

According to this writer, God does not expect us to attain sinless perfection; if He did, we would be doomed to a life of failure and frustration. Personal perfection is not His goal at all. What He wants most is for us to grow in love--love for Him and love for others--that we might be more like Jesus. To that end God has given us the Bible, full of insight and counsel on the way to overcome every temptation that we could possibly face and to develop good habits instead.

The Apostle Paul called these "exceedingly great and precious promises" that through these you may partake of the divine nature (2 Peter 1:4). Thus, God's word, combined with the miracle-working power of the Holy Spirit and sincere desire to make positive changes, can turn any weak point one may have into a strong one.

Most serious and committed Christians have learned that the Bible is a unique book, unique because it is the revelation of God's view of life. God communicates His perspective to us through Scripture in four ways, as explained by Bellis and McDowell (1982):

1. He teaches us His principles
2. He reproves us of wrong
3. He corrects our responses to restore us to fellowship
4. He trains us in patterns of proper living

Remember, the Bible was written over a period of 1,500 years by more than 40 authors and in circumstances which were highly diverse. God used each of these men, with their different viewpoints, abilities, conditioning, and time periods, to record scripture. What a diverse group! Yet, when compared, each of their individual writings exhibits perfect harmony and continuity with the others.

Not only was the Bible written by a variety of authors of different occupations, mood, condition and place, but it was also written on three different continents: Asia, Africa and Europe. It was written in three different languages: Hebrew (most of the Old Testament), Aramaic (portions of Daniel), and Greek (all of the New Testament). Yet, when the books of the Bible are compared, they perfectly harmonize in theme and purpose. No other book, ancient or modern, has such "credentials." According to McDowell and Bellis (1982), this is one verification of its supernatural authorship.

There is no doubt that the Bible was written for our benefit as spelt out from the Scripture as indicated in the following passages: Psalms 102:18 (The Living Bible): "I am recording this so that future generations will also praise the Lord for all that He has done. And a people that shall be created shall praise the Lord." And in John 19:35: "I saw all this myself and have given an accurate report so that you can believe."

Another benefit of the Bible for the Christian is recorded in John 20:30-31: Jesus' disciples saw him do many other miracles besides the ones told about in this book, but these are recorded so that you will believe that He is the Messiah, the Son of God, and that believing in Him you will have life. These things that were written in the Scriptures so long ago are to teach us patience and to encourage us so that we will look forward expectantly to the time when God will conquer sin.

According to First Corinthians 10:11, all things happened to the early writers to serve as examples--as object lessons to us--to warn us against making the same mistakes as the authors of the Bible had

4

made; they were written down so that we may read them and learn from them in these last days as the world nears its end.

Let us examine now the ways in which the Christian and his Bible respond to the challenges facing contemporary Nigeria. A simple definition of the word "contemporary" is "living and occurring at the same time," while a "challenge" questions or stimulates the way we do things. To understand the challenges or problems that face Christians in Nigeria today, there is need for us to understand our changing world. The Apostle Paul, in Rom. 13:11-14 and 2nd Tim. 3:1-5 and 4:1-5, reminds us to understand our contemporary world.

In addition, we are admonished that a reason for right living is the fact that we know how late it is; time is running out. The coming of the Lord is nearer now than when we first believed. We must understand our world so that we are aware of the temptations which it offers. We must be decent and true so that our behavior will be an example to others. We must ask the Lord Jesus to help us live in these difficult days when it is growing ever more challenging to be a Christian.

With the Bible as our guide, we must preach the Word of God urgently at all times, whenever we have an opportunity, when it is convenient and when it is not. We are called to correct each other, to encourage each other to do right, and at all times be feeding from and sharing the Word. For there is coming a time when people will not listen to the truth, but will go around looking for teachers who will tell them just what they want to hear. They will not listen to the message of the Bible, but will blithely follow their own misguided ideas.

If we are true Christians, we are called to stand steady and to be unafraid of suffering for the Lord. We are called to bring others to Christ, to leave nothing undone that we ought to have done (2 Tim. 4:1-5). The warnings given by Paul in these passages are very timely and relevant to present day Nigeria. Certainly in the 21st century, Nigeria is in need of change. It is hard, as Stearns (2009) points out, to read the headlines each day without a growing sense of alarm. Most recently we hear of the terrorism being inflicted by the group Boko Haram. Ethnic and religious tensions abound, corrupt governments create havoc, natural disasters uproot homes and businesses, climate change causes never before heard of problems, and a host of other problems challenge not only our Nigeria, but the world at large. As Stearns says, the post 9/11 world is both frightening and threatening and the majority of people struggle to understand it, let alone have clear ideas how to react to it.

The problems within Nigeria--and the world-- seem too large for most of us, even for those of us who call ourselves Christian. It is easier to retreat from them than to take them on. On Sunday mornings as we sit safe in our church pews and surrounded with friends, it can be all too easy to leave the violence, suffering and turmoil outside--out of sight and out of mind.

But wait--as Christians are we given the option of turning away from the problems that plague our communities and our nation? Does God permit that? Our personal faith in Jesus Christ requires much more than having just a personal and transforming relationship with God; it also entails a public and transforming relationship with the contemporary world. If our personal faith in Christ has no positive outward expression, then, as Stearns stresses, our faith is unfulfilled.

Christians in contemporary Nigeria must look to the Bible to bring a message of hope in these perilous times--the message of the almighty power of God's presence and the ways in which His children can lay hold of that power. The Scriptures provide endless examples of the ways the presence of the Lord empowers His people to live for Him. One of the most relevant examples is the life of Moses. Wilkerson, in a message delivered in Times Square, New York City, on March 2, 2009, explained that Moses was convinced that without God's presence in his life, it was useless for him to attempt anything. When Moses spoke face to face with the Lord, he stated boldly, "If your presence does not go with us, do not send us up from here." (Exodus 33:15) He was saying, "Lord, if you're not with us, we're not going to make it. We won't take a single step until we are assured of your presence."

Moses knew that it was God's presence among them that set them apart from all other nations. The same is true of Christians in Nigeria today. The only thing that sets us apart from the contemporary world is the dependence upon our Bible and God's presence among us, leading us, guiding us, working His will in and through us. His presence drives out fear, frustration and confusion.

The attitude of Moses was that we operate on one principle alone. The only way for us to be guided or governed, to do battle and survive these times, is to study the Bible and to be assured of His presence with us. When His presence is in our midst, no one can destroy us. Without Him we are helpless, reduced to nothing and completely open to the evils of the world. In Exodus 33:14, God answers Moses' bold statement: "My presence will go with you, and I will give you rest." (The Hebrew word for "rest" here means "a comfortable, peaceful confidence.") God is saying, "No matter what battles or trials you face, you will always be able to find a quiet rest and confidence in me."

His instruction to Moses, and to Christians in any society, in any time period remains the same: "Meditate upon the laws I have given you and pass them on to our children. These laws are not mere words--they are your life. Through obeying them you will live long, plentiful lives. . ." (Deu. 32:46-47) Moses instructed his people to meditate on the Word because of what that Word would do for them during their pilgrimage in the wilderness. Christians in Nigeria should know what the Bible, the Word of God, does for them also.

In summary, the Word saves us and gives us spiritual rebirth as explicitly explained in Psalms 19:7a, James 1:18 and 1:21b, 1 Peter 1:23, and 2 Peter 1:1-4. The Word gives us faith, truth, wisdom and strength (Rom.10:17, Psalms 19:7b, Psalms 119:99-100, John 15:7, Acts 20:32, and 2 Tim. 3:15-17). Meditating on the Word brings prosperity and success (Joshua 1:8, Psalms 1:2-3, 1 Tim 4:15). The Word guides us and is a light to our path (Psalms 19:8, 25:10,

119:105, 130). Finally, the Word cleanses us spiritually (Psalms 119:9, John 15:3, and Eph. 5:25b-26).

As Christians in Nigeria face trials, temptations, and persecution today, we should be able to say with pride, "I am not ashamed of the gospel because it is the power of God for the salvation of everyone who believes." (Rom. 1:16) And it is upon that Gospel that Christians base their lives as they face today's challenges, personal, within the community, within Nigeria, and the world.

Because of the force of the Spirit within us, we believe that when the world seems to be shaking, there will arise a people who know how to maintain their strength and integrity in the midst of it all. These are people who draw near to the Lord in times of crisis--and at all times--by keeping in touch with their Bible through studying the Word. According to Scripture, it will not matter to these people if the moon and stars fall from the sky, or if the mountains quake and fall into the sea, or if persecution and corruption abound. They will still have faith in the Lord to save them, and they will not have their faith shaken by anything that comes.

If we hope to stand steadfast in the storms and challenges of the contemporary world, the Scripture's counsel is simple: The Christian must have the Lord's presence in his life daily. Holding fast to the Word and to prayer is the single answer for the Christian in the midst of the turmoil of 21st century Nigeria.

CHAPTER TWO

The Christian Family in Contemporary Nigeria

The family is the cornerstone in any society. Without strong family relationships, the community cannot function fully; this is especially true in Christian communities, where committed individuals recognize the importance of Biblical teachings as they raise children to be responsible citizens. Thus, in addressing the question of challenges to Nigeria's society, we must look first to the structure of the family and the ways in which it may meet and respond to these challenges.

The "moral" upbringing of children is a first consideration. A child in most traditional societies is any person who has not reached the age of physical maturity. Most boys mature at the age of 15 and girls at 13. However, parents in most modern nations, including Nigeria, must realize that even at the age of 18, children still need help from their parents, relatives, and the community if they are to become fulfilled and responsible adults.

The word "moral" has to do with right and wrong behavior and character. "Get rid of all moral filth and evil that is so prevalent, and humbly accept the Word of God which can save you," is the admonition found in James 1:21. It is also explained as behavior which follows exactly that which society considers good or acceptable. These explanations reveal how the moral upbringing of a child could include training in customs, manners, or patterns of behavior that conform to the standards of a particular group.

Murray (1973), in explaining the importance of moral upbringing states the following:

> Cultivate every mental power, keeping in view the preparation of a sharp instrument for the Master's use. Cultivate natural virtues--diligence and decision, order and method, promptness and firmness--with the high aim of the child more fit for work to be done. Cultivate every moral power to be the form prepared for the Holy Spirit's filling. Let obedience to conscience and to law, let self-control and temperance, let strict integrity and justice, let humility and love, be the aim in education. . . and the upbringing of a child.

The above elaborates upon the need for and importance of moral development and the formation of moral values in the growing child. But what exactly are "moral" values? The term may be explained by reference to the term "morality," which comes from the Latin, "moralis," meaning "customs, manners, or patterns of behavior that conform to the standards of the group." These judgments lead society to label a person as "moral" or "immoral," depending on the extent to which he conforms.

Bhatia and Bhatia (1986), in their explanations on these moral judgments, express the idea that such judgments depend on the extent to which the expectations are met according to rules, customs, and traditions of the social group. If the individual obeys the rules and laws of society, he is considered "moral." At times, he may not totally agree with those laws and rules, but he may conform to them because that is the only course open to him. Accordingly, some people choose to do the "right" thing because it causes the least harmful results to him. If the individual acts according to the rules and laws of society because of controls from within himself, then he is known as a morally mature person.

On the other hand, the "immoral" person is one who fails to conform to group expectations as defined by rules, customs and laws. This person does not conform, not because of ignorance of these expectations, but rather because he feels no obligation to the group, nor does he approve of the standards of behavior expected by the group.

The moral upbringing of a child does not happen by chance. It comes through disciplined, deliberate effort by parents and society. The Bible tells us that no one is good except God, and that we are by nature sinful and unclean. In fact, there is no evidence to prove the prevailing belief that a person is born "good" or "bad" in the sense that he acts or does not act according to the rules of the society to which he belongs. (Mason, 1982) On the other hand, there is much religious and psychological evidence that morality is learned. Like all learning, according to Bhatia and Bhatia, morality can be controlled and directed so that an individual will attain the ability to act according to the expectations of the society in which he lives.

We should understand that the process of becoming a moral person begins early in childhood and continues through the years of adolescence. True moral behavior is that which comes from within rather than from fears from the outside. Writers like Bhatia and Bhatia have suggested that there are six phases in the development of moral behavior in the young:

1. Learning impulse control
2. Learning moral rules and principles
3. Learning motives and attitudes from people who are near to him
4. Forming an ideal self as early as five or six years of age as a model to imitate; this ideal self may change as the individual ages, but it is a valuable guide
5. Forming a scale of values

6. Reaching the ability to apply moral principles to new
   situations

Moral attitudes and values learnt during the upbringing of a child often change as the adolescent meets people having different attitudes and values. But the foundations laid earlier in the process of upbringing usually persist.

It is important to recognize that the most important learning in the cultivation of morality takes place in the home, the Church, the Mosque, and the social group. Frequently, the learning in the home emphasizes the negative aspects of moral behavior, i.e., what should not be done, or acts to avoid. In times past, education was the business of the Temple, Church or Mosque, and moral education was imparted through direct teaching based on religious scriptures. Gradually, first in Western cultures and then in the East--Africa and even in Nigeria, especially in Borno State--religious education has given place to secularism in most state-supported schools, and moral education has been relegated to a very minor position.

We must understand that moral education or upbringing consists not only of teaching the individual moral codes of the group, but also of instilling in the child a high regard for these values so that he may be willing to accept them and to direct his behavior in accordance with them. It is absolutely necessary that the growing child learn to control his behavior himself, so that external controls will not be needed; this will be of benefit to the child and also to the social group. As the child becomes an adult, he will be responsible for his own actions, and will no longer have to rely on parents and teachers to tell him what and what not to do. The child will be able to decide for himself and act according to those decisions, not only for his own benefit, but for the benefit of others.

The Holy Bible in Ephesians 4:23-24 (The Living Bible) states that one's attitudes and thoughts must all be constantly changing for the better. We are to be new and different, holy and good. We are to clothe ourselves with this new nature. By inference we see from this Scripture that there are certain moral concepts which a child should form; he should have definite attitudes regarding them and have clear ideas about behavior in situations relating to them. Such situations might include honesty as opposed to cheating, lying, stealing, destructiveness, drinking, drug habits, etc., and responsibility and cooperation as opposed to sex offences, cruelty, and lack of respect. Both the home and the school should provide situations in which these areas are discussed and the child should be encouraged to express opinions on them.

Quoting further from The Living Bible, Ephesians 4:25-31: "Stop lying to each other; tell the truth, for we are parts of each other and when we lie to each other we are hurting ourselves. If you are angry, don't sin by nursing your grudge. Don't let the sun go down with you still angry--get over it quickly, for when you're angry you give a mighty foothold to the devil.

If anyone is stealing, he must stop it and begin using those hands of his for honest work so he can give to others in need. Don't use bad language. Say only what is good and helpful to those you are talking to, and what will give them a blessing. Stop being mean, bad tempered and angry, quarrelling, using harsh words; and dislike of others should have no place in your lives. Instead be kind to each other, tenderhearted, forgiving one another, just as God has forgiven you because you belong to Christ."

We are further instructed in the same Book, Chapter 5, to follow God's example in everything we do, including in the moral upbringing of our children. Specific instructions are given: "Let there be no sex sin, impurity or greed among you. Let no one be able to accuse you of such things. Dirty stories, foul talk, coarse jokes-- these are not for you. Instead, remind each other of God's goodness and be thankful. Take no part in the worthless pleasures of evil and darkness, but instead, rebuke and expose them. It would be shameful even to mention here those pleasures of darkness which the ungodly do. But when you expose them, the light shines in upon their sin and shows it up, and when they see how wrong they really are, some of them may even become children of light."

Through the years, people have subtly undercut the importance of sexual morality, honesty, personal integrity, and meaningful faith in God. Sexual irresponsibility for some people has suddenly become dignified in our society, to the shame of parents, religious leaders, and Nigerian society in general.

There is, however, some hope, because not everyone has allowed passion to overrule judgment. There are those who still believe that sexual irresponsibility carries an enormous price tag for the momentary pleasure it promises. Despite the "reasoning" philosophy of Hugh Heffner and his Playmates in America, Dobson (1984) explains that sexual freedom is a direct thoroughfare to disillusionment, emptiness, divorce, venereal diseases of all kinds, AIDS, illegitimacy, and broken lives. Not only do promiscuous individuals suffer adverse consequences, history reveals that entire societies begin to deteriorate when free "love" reaches a position of social acceptance.

This fact, according to Dobson, was first illuminated by J.D. Unwin, a British social anthropologist who spent seven years studying the births and deaths of eight civilizations. He reported from his exhaustive research that every known culture in the world's history has followed the same sexual pattern; during its early days in existence, premarital and extramarital relationships were strictly prohibited. Great creative energy was associated with this inhibition of sexual expression, causing the culture to prosper. Much later in the life of the society, its people began to rebel against the strict prohibitions, demanding the freedom to release their internal passions. As the mores weakened, the social energy abated, eventually resulting in the decay or destruction of the civilization.

Dr. Unwin (1984) explains that the energy which holds a society together is sexual in nature. When a man is devoted to one woman and one family, he is motivated to build, save, protect, plan and prosper on their behalf. However, when his sexual interests are dispersed and generalized, his effort is invested in the gratification of sensual desires. Unwin concludes that human society is forced either to display great energy or to enjoy sexual freedom; the evidence is that they cannot do both for more than one generation. Nigeria is not likely to be the first to fulfill these opposing purposes.

Most people believe in moral decency and would want to instill responsible sexual attitudes in their children. Parents and teachers who fall in the same shoes should know that this task is not an easy one. The sexual urge is stronger during adolescence than in any other period in life, and there is no way to guarantee that an independent teenager will choose to control it. It is impossible, and probably undesirable, to shield the child from the permissive attitudes that are prevalent today: television, video, internet, motion pictures all bring every element of the sexual revolution into the sanctuary of one's home. Thus, solitary confinement of the child is not the answer. Furthermore, there is a danger that parents and teachers will make one mistake in their efforts to avoid another. While attempting to teach discipline in matters of morality, they must be careful not to inculcate attitudes that will interfere with sexual fulfillment in future marital relations.

The task of forming healthy moral attitude and understanding in children requires considerable skill and tact, and parents are often keenly aware of their lack of preparation for this assignment. If children are to learn what society expects of them, and if they are to be prepared to take their place productively in that society, they must have a solid moral background within the family. Their upbringing should include these three important components of discipline: education in moral precepts, rewards for socially approved behavior, and appropriate punishment for doing wrong by intention.

Other aspects include a child's respect for his parents. That is to say that his attitude toward the leadership of his parents is critical to his acceptance of their values and philosophy, including their concept of sexual behavior. The most fundamental element in teaching morality can be achieved through a healthy parent-child relationship during the early years when it is vitally important that parents lead by example, modeling the kind of attitudes and behavior that they are attempting to inculcate in their children. Parents should be trustworthy, supportive, and caring as well as sensitive to the child's needs, feelings, and interests. Mutual respect must be developed. Teaching the young child to choose the right path will help to ensure that when he is older he will remain upon it.

The moral upbringing of children is not an easy task, especially when our children are immersed in a world where all too often they are exposed to the very behaviors we wish them to avoid. Contemporary society in Nigeria cries out for a return to the moral attributes of honesty, compassion, integrity; a society lacking in these will not be successful in meeting the challenges that confront it. Children are the hope of the future of the family, of the community, and of the nation; it is the responsibility of all parents to lead by example in raising their children so that they are prepared to meet these challenges.

CHAPTER THREE

The Importance of the Pastor and Theological Education

If the foundation of a Christian community is the teachings of the Bible, surely one of the most significant sources of leadership in that community is the pastor and his education in theology. Therefore, let us consider the importance of theological education in facing the challenges of the 21st century in Nigeria.

We recognize first that the emergence of new religions, faiths and movements in the light of the post-modern era has directly or indirectly challenged the nucleus of theological education, not only in Nigeria, but globally as well. While there is need for frequent change in the curricula within these institutions, the message of Christ which they teach remains a constant.

The basis of theological education is rooted in Scripture and centers around the acknowledgment that "the fear of God is the beginning of wisdom." (Prov. 1:7) Education in Scripture starts from the home. (Deut. 6:6-9) Parents are admonished to instruct their children in their earliest years. This early theological training was what sustained, transformed and developed Israel and many other nations of the world. We cannot afford to underestimate this humble beginning.

In the broadest sense, education in any field involves more than the cognitive domain; it is also affective, involving the shaping of values, attitudes, and emotions. Knowledge without passion, according to Paul, amounts to nothing. The greatest commandment sets the standard for our passions. The task of theological education is to teach the love of God and love of neighbor. Problem-posing education requires empathy, understanding issues with both mind and heart. It is not simply an academic exercise, but a spirit-filled identification with God and His people that empowers those people to action. The 21st century theological educator will need to guide (rather than indoctrinate) his students in shaping their affections, sorting out their values, and acting on their commitments in the power of the Spirit. (Wanak, 2008) In the words of Derek (1979), "Education--theological or otherwise--aims at developing the individual's aptitude for every kind of learning so that they are well informed, equipped, quick to understand, and qualified for service."

Turning to the Biblical basis, Prime, in his enthusiasm for education, notes that in the book of Proverbs, "Education aims at imparting understanding (4:1,7), knowledge (15:14) and wisdom." (2:1-6, 14:33) These aims are instrumental in producing a morally and ethically balanced society that would ensure the viable and sustainable development of a nation. The New Testament, too, builds on these values with the same purpose. And so it was with the early Church, until the Reformation period which championed free access to scripture and contributed immensely to the development of theological education in the 16th century.

Such development gave birth to scholasticism in a positive manner. The Church became so learned, seeking to alleviate the sufferings of the poor and the uneducated at every opportunity. The secular (non-religious) society was then prompted to innovate and build her own principles of education apart from those of the Church.

The Middle Ages was also the period of theologians and clergy. While clergy influenced the affairs of both kings and the common folk, theology became the queen of sciences. Europe and America were built on these Christian principles, but today theological education in both Europe and America is in serious crisis because the curriculum contents fail to address the problems prompted by prevailing secularism. It is sad to hear of liberals and indeed liberal theologians confessing, "We are living in a post-Christian era." Theologians in Nigeria must learn the lessons from this departure; otherwise, we will become victims of this great shift in thinking.

Theological education in the 20th century had been dominated by the West with its theological categories shaped by Greek culture, its educational patterns shaped by the university world, its attitudes influenced by modernity, industrialism, colonialism, and individualism. In the past, its spirituality was marked by pietism (devotion and reverence to God); in the present, it bears a faith of affluence and superficial commitment, and as the 20th Century came to a close, the zeal of the Western Church was waning (Wanak, 2008).

There are many forces that influence the shape of theological education in the present century. Today there are more Christians in the two-thirds worlds than in the West. Churches among the developing nations are growing, as are its theological institutions. Asia claims the largest seminary in the world, Chongshin University in Korea. The Philippines boast of over 300 Bible schools and seminaries, while Africa has well over 800 seminaries.

What will theological education look like at the end of the 21st century, when these seminaries and others yet to be founded begin to dominate the theological scene? How will the Christian faith be re-contextualized? How will it be prepared to assist families, communities and the nation in meeting the challenges confronting them?

As we consider these questions, we note that one of the beautiful aspects of theological education as it has functioned so far in this century has been its emphasis on Biblical knowledge as an indispensable part of the training process. Without that, one cannot enjoy personal spiritual growth in godly character, nor can effective and meaningful ministry to others ensue if the foundation of the message of the Bible is not uppermost in training for the pastoral ministry. According to MacArthur (2005), Sola Scriptura and Sola fide (the Scriptures alone and faith alone) provide the mortar binding together the building blocks of ministry. Miller (1812) observed that "in addition to piety and ability, those called to the pastoral ministry must have a 'competent knowledge,' without which both piety and talents united are inadequate to the official work."

As expressed by MacArthur, no movement can impact a society with its creed if its leaders are ignorant of or continually undermining the veracity and applicability of its charter documents. Henry rightly contended that the one book above all others in which a twentieth century scholar should be learned remains the Bible; among the great books with which one should be familiar, the Bible stands tallest. The Church today needs nothing so much as a vital recovery of the authority and comprehensive truthfulness of scripture and its applications to all dimensions of life.

This aspect of theological training should not be taken lightly. The influence of the teacher upon the pupil is enormous, not only in what is taught, but also in how it is taught. (Luke 6:40) Consequently, biblical and theological mentors must pass the scrutiny of 1 Tim. 3:1-7 and Titus 1:5-9 if they are to prepare others effectively. The ministerial qualifications and pastoral experience of the teacher are vital factors in the educational equation, according to MacArthur. He further stresses that being biblically knowledgeable and theologically accurate should derive motivation first and foremost from a yearning to know God intimately. (Phil. 3:8-10)

In "Knowing God," Packer (1993) writes:

> To be preoccupied with getting theological knowledge as an end in itself, to approach Bible study with no higher a motive than a desire to know all the answers, is the direct route to a state of self-satisfied self-deception. . . There can be no spiritual health with doctrinal knowledge; but it is equally

true that there can be no spiritual health with it, if
it is sought for the wrong purpose and valued by
the wrong standard. . . We must seek, in studying
God, to be led by God. It was for this purpose that
revelation was given, and it is to this use that we
must put it.

Dietrich Werner, ETE/WCC (1997), explains that Theological
education is vital for the transmission of Christian tradition form
one generation to the other. It is essential for the renewal and
continuity of the Church and its leadership. Theological education
is a matter of survival for an authentic and contextual mission of the
Church in contemporary contexts. Theological education is crucial
for the interaction between Church and society, where many issues
demand for a sharpened stand and passion of Christianity. This has
become a common conviction in Western and Eastern Churches, in
Christianity of the South and Christianity of the North.

Ecumenical theological education and broad-base ecumenical
formation is a vital priority for Christianity in the 21st century and
the continuation of the ecumenical movement as was affirmed by
the last assembly of the world council of Churches in PortoAlegre.
Without an increased commitment towards the ecumenical agenda
(in its broad understanding), the unity of the Church and its holistic
mission and service in today's world in theological education we
might see an increased fragmentation of world Christianity, we
might see growing trends of religious fundamentalism and a severe
lack of properly trained Christian leadership for many fast growing
Churches in the Southern Hemisphere.

Another important effect of theological education in the 21st
century is the desire for a commitment or requirement by theological
educators to study the scriptures historically, and a seminary's
demand that theology, ethics, mission, preaching and pastoral care
all flow out of sound exegetical, or critically interpretive, conclusions.
Winning through grinding work of reading the Bible in its original

languages and historical contexts will appear to many to be elitist, filled with the pride of intellectualism. To others it will appear too time-consuming, impractical and irrelevant in the face of serious issues that surround us. Still others will argue that such a scripture-centered curriculum strikes at the heart of an egalitarianism that many falsely equate with the Gospel and our cherished Protestant heritage. Only those seminaries that can communicate their "unpopular" convictions clearly and persuasively with prospective students and with the Church in a sort of "pre-education" will overcome the initial shock of such a rigorous and old fashioned approach to theological studies. (Hafemann, 1988)

A further effect is in the area of theological framework. Theology is often defined as that which is known about God through the self-disclosure of Himself, primarily through the Scriptures (i.e., special revelation) but also in creation (general revelation). This, according to MacArthur (2005) has three rudimentary elements that comprise a proper theological framework or grid through which one filters what he reads and hears: historical theology, biblical theology, and systematic theology. He further explains that historical theology provides invaluable insight into the issues, debates, councils, and creeds in church history. It also demonstrates how the teaching of Scripture has formulated and shaped into dogmas, creeds, and confessions of faith.

Biblical theology, on the other hand, in a narrow sense, provides the student with basic understanding of each biblical author, book, or group of books. Quality training must include a study of these elements, providing an essential picture of pieces that make up the whole.

Warfield (1978) notes the significance of such a study:

> Its exegetical value lies just in this circumstance, that it is only when we have thus concatenated an author's theological statements into a whole that we can be sure that we understand them as

he understood them in detail. A light is inevitably thrown back from Biblical theology upon the separate theological deliverances as they occur in the text, such as subtly colors them, and often for the first time, gives them to us in their true setting, and thus enables us to guard against perverting them when we adapt them to our use.

The third element of the theological framework, which is systematic theology, collects the pieces and puts them together into a whole. This, as Warfield points out, is an outgrowth of historical and biblical theology, being fed, tested, and collected by a constant infusion of exegesis/interpretation as exhibited in biblical theology. It is this that provides an ordered summary or synopsis of important themes in biblical teaching, assembled in such a way as not to violate the contexts of the individual parts.

A rise in the level of education is another effect of theological education in this century; the average annual increase in enrolment of students is quite substantial. This shows clearly that today students will be more highly educated, and the curricula and teaching methods will have to be prepared to meet the needs of these more sophisticated students.

In addition, there is a global trend toward equalizing gender privileges and roles, with a greater percentage of women entering theological institutions and the work force, as revealed in the UNESCO Yearbook statistics. This trend, as Wanak (2008) asserts, will challenge traditional views concerning the role of women in the Church; thus, theological institutions will need to address the implications of a more gender-equal society. For some, this will require the painful process of re-examining past beliefs and forming new ones.

Johnstone, in his 5th revised edition of "Operations World" (1993), shows clearly that globally the growth rate of evangelicals is due largely to conversion as opposed to population growth. Although

Islam is the fastest growing religion, it is growing at a lesser rate than the population growth of its adherents. According to this author, non-evangelical Protestants show a negative growth rate.

Another area that must be mentioned is urbanization. Theological educators of the 21st century, more than ever before, will need to think in terms of the city. As cities become increasingly diverse, educators will consider training in diversity in order to build dialogue, tolerance, respect, and understanding, without which evangelism will be fruitless. Faculties will definitely need to consider the ways in which students are to take their places in the world as citizen-believers without losing their distinctly Christian identity. (Wanak, 2005)

Theological education in Nigeria is currently undergoing a state of crisis according to Ndu (2006). The disarray in the academic programs of Nigerian theological institutions can only be likened to the picture of Israel in Judges 21:25: "In those days there was no king in Israel, every man did what was right in his own eyes." This is indeed evident in most curricula of our Bible schools, theological colleges, and seminaries. Ndu further observes that two main factors are primarily responsible for this crisis. First, there is the absence of a systematically and carefully articulated philosophy of theological education to guide both the development and the practice of the discipline in Nigeria; secondly, there is severe fragmentation of the enterprise among missions and denominational interests.

This fragmentation is an unfortunate development, and, as if that were not enough, the management of Nigerian theological institutions is in some cases still manned and keyed by missionaries. In this sense, these Nigerian theological institutions have no true voice because the webs of missionary imperialism still threaten the development of theological education in Nigeria as well as in the African continent. While it is true that theological education was started at almost the same time as secular education in Nigeria, the perennial crisis being experienced in our secular system still permits it to greatly overshadow the need of the theological.

There is an enormous task ahead. If we are to be functional in this enterprise, if we are to be assured of theological education that will produce men and women equipped to provide leadership in helping individuals, communities and the nation as they face the unprecedented demands of the modern world, we must first redefine our theological concept. Until we begin to see theology as a vehicle of change and transformation, and theology placed within a context of relevance, "true" theology cannot exist. Until our theological education curriculum is redefined and structured to meet the existential demands of our people and nation, theologians and theology will be irrelevant to our needs. We must overhaul the vestiges of the Western hermeneutical approach to scripture so as to pave the way for a more viable means of appropriating God's word in our particular Nigerian situation.

Until we see theology as a tool for reconciliation and a medium for propagating tolerance and acceptance in our doctrinal beliefs, we will not make an impact on our present generation. Until we learn from the history of the development of theological education and reaffirm our beliefs that this enterprise must begin from the home, through the Church, through society, we will fail to serve that society, and thus the nation. As Kolawole (2007) points out, "It is long overdue that theological education curriculum designed from the perspective of foreign culture but ironically for Nigerian and African socio-cultural setting be reviewed in order to meet indigenous requirements."

In the quest for self-identification and definition, he suggests that "The type of theological education curriculum that becomes a matter of necessity must emerge from a positive and rightly selected teamwork among Christian leaders saddled with the task of shaping theological curriculum relevant to the complex prevailing situation in Nigeria at the national level and Africa at the continental level." From these excerpts we can see the urgent need for concerted efforts to be made by theological institutions, departments of Christian religious studies in Nigerian universities, and other related higher institutions, in order to play their roles in making these vital changes a reality.

The effect of theological education in Nigeria cannot be overemphasized, for it cuts across the political, social, economic and cultural milieu of Nigerian society. For theological education to have meaningful impact in contemporary Nigeria, stakeholders must fully define the Nigerian context and the relevant theological disposition that will be suitable in bringing about positive results for society. Gone are the days when Western methodologies were used to teach scripture; we need methodologies that would critically define our context and at the same time ensure a greater relevance as we look to the ministry for vital help in meeting the current challenges to society.

One current issue relative to theological education is that in the 21st century, many of the post-World War II schools will seek accreditation. The question remains: how will school quality be measured? Accreditation is sometimes biased toward upper rail teaching and structures. Schools or seminaries with counterparts in the West, as expressed by Youngblood (1989), will more readily be accredited. Schools or seminaries addressing lower rail issues emphasizing cultural concerns and contextual ministerial needs will unfortunately have a more difficult time. With the strong emphasis on globalization, accreditation teams and school faculty must be vigilant in strengthening the lower rail emphasis in their curriculum, and in creating effective integration points.

Credentialing is also gaining prominence in many areas of theological education across the globe. Increasingly, faculty qualifications are coming under scrutiny. Theological institutions want their faculty to keep pace with national standards, and this naturally shifts the balance between academic, ministerial and spiritual formation, giving greater weight to academic concerns. Accreditation teams and school faculty will need to be vigilant in maintaining balance between these three areas of formation. Individual faculty members will need to keep current and to upgrade their own formal studies, in the biblical/spiritual as well as the academic realm. (Wanak, 2005)

As we have seen, the importance of theological education cuts across all strata of society: the political, the social, the economic. In the political context, the inseparability of religion and politics in Nigeria will be a viable means or tool for theological education to influence her citizens in their political ambition or focus because of the great potentials inherent in theological education, which with its God-given power, will influence man holistically. Man as a political being will use the cultural mandate very responsibly in governing the world in the way it is ordered by God. If we in this country need good governance and God's blessing, then the task of theological education must be embraced by all with all seriousness.

In the social context, theological education is a cornerstone in a morally decaying society like ours, where social vices and economic crimes are on increase. The social ills, which have eaten deeply into the very fabric of our lives, need to be addressed so that we can achieve the kind of development that would foster peace and a healthy environment for our peoples. Morality and ethics in this country have given way to Western secularism which has, in no small measure, challenged the very meaning of morality and ethics in the African/Nigerian context. If we do not want to see all kinds of sexual behaviors being "legalized," and all forms of social vices being perpetrated in our communities, we must facilitate the urgent training of theological educators in order to uphold our moral and ethical values at all levels, from the home to the Church and to the broader, national scene.

Considering the economic context, we are aware of the shameful acts of our corrupt leaders in this period of economic crisis. Corruption is a cancer that needs urgent attention; otherwise it will spread like wildfire. If we wish to experience development with all of its "positivisms," we must first define clearly our goals and agendas. We must also realize that that kind of enterprise demands hard work, integrity, influence, character building and above all the fear of God, which is the beginning of wisdom. (Prov. 1:7) Is not education in theology one of the underpinnings in establishing our goals and leading us to the kind of economic development we wish to see for our communities and our nation?

If the desired characteristics of Christian teachers in the 21st century are to be realized, we must draw from both biblical and modern scientific perspectives. Although we do not consider the Bible as a textbook, the Bible certainly tells us a great deal about essential qualities of Christian teachers and leaders; it teaches that godliness is the irreducible minimum criterion. Seminary students are influenced not only by the work within the classroom, but also by the out-of-class time spent with teachers and professors who should model the kind of behavior which encourages and supports leadership of integrity and godliness. The Bible enlightens us not only on essential qualities of Christian teachers; it also gives us models of excellence to follow as men of God taught the people of their day.

When we examine the issue from social science perspectives, we must remember that for teaching styles to be effective, they have to be in context and up to date. The social sciences as applied to education are of great benefit to the development of pedagogy. Educational psychology informs us about the developmental nature of people and about appropriate assessment procedures. Sociology helps us identify educational needs and contextual concerns. Curriculum theory guides the structure of learning. Instructional goals guide the teaching process, and instructional technology helps us package instruction for efficient use. (Wanak, 2005)

The task of the theological educator is to bridge the ancient text and the contemporary context, ancient pedagogy and modern approaches to academic, spiritual, and ministerial formation. The Holy Spirit is our guide in this process (1 Cor. 2:9-16), not only in the relationship of the text and the context, but also in the personal working out of those called to the ministry being both theologian and educator.

Considering that the task of 21st century educators, whether theological or strictly academic, is to prepare their students in addressing the issues which are plaguing our local societies as well as our nation, Chickering and Gamson (1991) suggest seven principles of good practice in education in general: That which encourages student-faculty contact, cooperation among students, active learning; which gives prompt feedback, emphasizes time on task, and communicates high expectations; and which respects diverse talents and ways of learning.

As explained by these writers, there are many roads to learning, because people bring differing talents and styles of learning to their classrooms. Brilliant students in the seminar room may be all thumbs in the laboratory. Students rich in hands-on experience may not do as well in theory. The seven principles, they further assert, raise several questions for theological education in the effort to increase its relevance for the present day needs:

1. Do students have adequate contact with faculty; are faculty involved in the lives of their students?
2. Are students involved in cooperative learning courses and extra-curricular activities within the community
3. Are discovery/inquiry methods of teaching being used to create active, self-directed learners?
4. Is productive feedback given to students without fear of damaging student/teacher relations or spoiling students with praise?
5. Are faculty well prepared and spending adequate time on the teaching/learning process?
6. Do teachers communicate high expectations of the students?
7. Are teachers prepared to accommodate many learning styles?

It is very important to understand that these questions are useful in evaluating the teaching-learning context. With the more sophisticated students of the 21st century, schools will need to hone their skills in these areas. Education, whether undergraduate or at the seminary level, must prove relevant to the needs of this century.

If the 20th century brought some unimaginable changes, the 21st century will be marked by acceleration of changes because of even more immediate, pressing and specific societal and national needs. Based on an acknowledgment and understanding of the issues facing the nation, theological institutions must first identify and make clear their vision, mission, values, and goals which are the useful tools in coordinating their efforts to achieve objectives which must be specific, measureable, and achievable.

Guiding these goals is a manifesto on The Renewal of Evangelical Theological Education developed by The International Council of Accrediting Agencies, as reported by Youngblood (1989). Core values and goals that theological institutions should seek to attain are as follows:

1. Contextualization
2. Churchward orientation
3. Strategic flexibility
4. Theological grounding
5. Continuous assessment
6. Community life
7. Integrated programming
8. Servant molding
9. Instructional variety
10. A Christian mind
11. Equipping for growth

There are many requirements in the pursuit of these goals: helping faculty identify strengths and weaknesses and ways to work through plans for continuous improvement, creation of mechanisms for accurate student evaluation, development of in-service programs, improving credentials, developing the institution's organizational culture, and seeking funding for the institutions by creating financial links.

All of the above stresses the importance of bringing theological education up to date so that it can provide the ministerial leadership so sorely needed in this time of corruption, violence, and social unrest. Homes, communities, and the nation are looking to this leadership so that the future will be bright with the promise of our God-given legacy.

CHAPTER FOUR

The Challenge in Addressing Religious Violence and Providing Conflict Resolution in Northern Nigeria

Religious violence is presenting the current single greatest challenge to Nigerian society, especially in the North, with the uprising of the terrorist group, Boko Haram. Before we turn to that specific threat, however, let us examine the idea of religious violence and conflict resolution in general as it applies to our nation.

Religious violence, according to Wikipedia encyclopedia, is a term that covers all phenomena where religion, in any of its forms, is the subject of either individual or collective violent behavior. It covers violence by religiously motivated individuals or religious institutions of any kind, of the same religion, of a different sect, or secular targets. There is also violence of any kind against objects that are explicitly religious, such as religious institutions, buildings or sites, and the persecution of people on the basis of their religious beliefs.

Religious violence, it further explains, like all violence, is an inherently cultural process whose meanings are dependent upon context. It may be worth noting that religious violence often tends to place great emphasis on the symbolic aspect of the act. It is primarily the domain of the violent "actor," which may be distinguished between individuals and collective forms of violence (James, Kyoko, Tokuno, and Wellman, 2004).

There are two types of violence that are closely related when speaking or writing about religious violence. The first is ritual violence, which may be directed against victims (human sacrifice, ritual murder) or self-inflicted (religious self-flagellation). The second, collective religious violence, is what we more commonly picture when we think of religious violence. The term "collective" refers to any violent activity that is perpetrated within the context of society, is legitimized by at least a subset of society or religion, and always has a political dimension. It should be noted that the term "collective" does not mean that a single individual cannot undertake collective religious violence.

Serious religious violence in most instances is perpetrated by individuals belonging to groups whose religious zeal and conviction exceed that of an average member of the wider society, although milder forms, such as verbal abuse or ostracism, can be habitually practiced by larger communities. Even though religion is used to justify violent behavior, the immediate motivations of individuals involved may not necessarily be religious as such, and the goals of such behavior may be cultural, personal, or political, social or even economical. In the case of the violence recently being committed by Boko Haram, motivation may be a mix of political and religious.

Increasing Islamic militancy and other religious violence and conflicts connected to religion have claimed many lives and properties of both Christians and Muslims in Nigeria. Even the church leadership and rank and file are beginning to question: Are there limits to Pacifism? The pacifist stance of some churches such as the Ekklesiyar Yan'uwa A Nigeria (EYN), per se, is not in question, but Christian communities on the front line are looking for practical answers in terms of what can be considered legitimate self-defense. For that they need to rely on the police, civil defense corps, and the armed forces of the state.

Traditionally, Jesus' teaching in the New Testament against

violence and retaliation has been the foundation of the Pacifist position and is the bulwark of its ethical stance. But peacemakers need to understand that in many ways, often subtle and hidden, even sometimes open, injustice disturbs and destroys peace. Peace is always shattered when people of power and privilege use that for personal, political, or economic gain. How can the Church in a country like Nigeria practice total pacifism or have peace when some live lavishly while many starve, where civil rights are trampled upon and citizens are exploited in personal relationships, where one person or group in the name of religion dominates, uses, and abuses others? Such injustice breeds violence--and the Bible sees it as violence because the humanity and God's image of persons are violated by it. (Hoogerwerf, et al., 1983)

It is unfortunate that Nigeria, a country known to be religious in nature, has over the years destroyed the very essence of religion through so many religious conflicts that could have been avoided. As expressed by Hall (1997), conflict is the inevitable paradox or corollary of human existence and civilization. For prosperity in life and society, according to Hall, man intervenes in nature by way of exploration and exploitation in order to produce the material aspects of existence. He asserts further that this phenomenon can be traced back to the beginnings of human society when individuals collaborated with one another through the use of simple tools, the rudimentary division of labor and the exchange of goods--all of which marked the beginnings of social organization.

Gofwen (2004), writing on the sources of religious conflict, identified religious intolerance as the major source of religious conflict in all societies as long as the history of mankind, permeating all forms of human civilization, with attendant destructive tendencies. According to him, no system could be found to be impervious to it, because deeper cleavages are created in society by religious intolerance than by any other factor. Several factors are responsible for this lack of tolerance, the first of which is the lack of capacity in a society to harmonize conflicting and mutually intolerant religious

beliefs. In this case, religion becomes a divisive force, as typified by the existence of both Islam and Christianity.

The second factor is the diversity of interpretations of doctrine within the same religion. And the third factor responsible for religious intolerance has its source in conversion campaigns. Indoctrination, yielding to religious fanaticism is also a corollary ideological force accompanying this development and process, as exemplified in both Christian and Moslem schools where children receive primarily either one of the two forms of religious education.

It should also be noted that the desperation of economically disenfranchised people in this country is ventral to conflicts, and must be taken seriously in considering any of the solutions to the larger problem of religious violence. This violence in Nigeria seems to defy all suggestions, recommendations, or solutions to this cancer which has brought untold hardship and destruction to our democracy, our economy, our development, our political maturity.

In his work, "The Shadow of Religion on Nigerian Federalism: 1960-93," J.I. Elaigwu (1993) has given a summary of violent religious incidences taking place within those dates; following that summary, the years 2001-2008 are listed, with information taken from The News, December 15, 2008. It is clear that conflict resolution must be part of any approach to violence of any kind. Wikipedia, the free encyclopedia, explains "conflict resolution" as a range of processes aimed at alleviating or eliminating sources of conflict, and states that the term is sometimes used interchangeably with "dispute resolution" or "alternative dispute resolution." Others since late 1980's prefer to use conflict "transformation" because of certain questions and concerns, and even suspicions about what such concepts mean, because quick solutions to deep socio-political problems would not change things in any significant way, i.e., transformation, real change, must take place before a conflict can be eliminated; the word "resolution" may imply more of a "quick fix" with results that may be only temporary.

Processes of conflict resolution generally include negotiation,

mediating, counseling and diplomacy. According to Wikipedia, the processes of arbitration, litigation, and formal complaint processes such as ombudsman intervention, are usually described with the term dispute resolution, although some refer to them as conflict resolution. The processes of mediation and arbitration, on the other hand, are often referred to as dispute resolution.

Don Helder Camara, a Brazilian church leader and defender of the poor, attempts to aid modern peacemakers in understanding the biblical connection between injustice and violence. He writes about the "spiral of violence" which traps both oppressors and the oppressed in a continuing cycle of conflict, be it religious or ethnic.

Camara (1983) identifies three kinds of violence that fuel the vicious spiral. The first is injustice. Land owned by peasant farmers is seized by the government and sold to a corporation which hires the peasants to work the land at wages so low that their families suffer malnutrition, disease and death. Or racist policies force minority youth to endure poor housing, inferior schools, poverty and high unemployment. Or security police seize people and hold them without trial. This first form of violence, Camara explains, is often called "invisible violence" because only the victims are aware of it. Physical or religious conflict need not be involved. The violence is institutional. The unjust structures of a society violate the humanity and well-being of some people in it.

Because oppressed people seek the same freedom most enjoy, injustice breeds a second form of violence--revolts, strikes, demonstrations, etc. These are usually taken advantage of by hoodlums under the guise of religion, tribe, or politics. In such cases, the authorities usually respond to revolts or strikes with a third form of violence: repression. The army or secret police move in to crush the labor union, arrest protesters, or do battle with revolutionaries. This violence, Camara asserts, attempts to restore "law and order" and return to the status quo, with no resolution taking place. This repression usually involves even greater injustice which ignites further violence. (Don Helder Camara, The Spiral of

Violence, from Christ is Our Peace by Koopman, Hoogerwerf, and White, 1993)

We know that this peace-making task in a country like Nigeria demands a great deal from all of us. We can respond by identifying those things which connect us as a people and recognizing the challenges and obstacles. We can listen to the cries of those who are oppressed because of their religion, tribe, or economic status; we can hear their message of helplessness and then share the ways we can all benefit from the gift of God by involvement in conflict resolution or transformation, by being involved in the political process, and by holding our politicians and leaders accountable for just policies and treatment for all.

Christians in Northern Nigeria especially, in the past and again in the present, have faced such violence and injustice. But God in His infinite mercy, power, love and grace keeps the Church growing in strength. He gives His people power to break the cycle of violence in our world--by showing our kindness, love, forgiveness, compassion, tolerance, and respect, and by employing dialogue and acts of justice.

An abstract on conflict resolution methods in The Wikipedia Encyclopedia informs us that there are many tools available to persons in times of conflict. The list is long: negotiation, mediation, community building, advocacy, diplomacy, activism, non-violence or pacifism, critical pedagogy, prayer, and counseling. How and when they are used depends on several factors, such as the specific issues at stake and the cultural context of the disputants.

In real world conflict situations, which range in scale from kindergarten bullying to genocide, practitioners will have to creatively combine several of these approaches as needed. Additionally, practitioners will often specialize in a particular scale (e.g., interpersonal, community, or international), or a particular variety of conflict (environmental, religious, or organizational). Those involved will use any repertoire of methods they find most useful. As indicated earlier, some experts prefer the term conflict

transformation, which promises that real change will take place, to conflict resolution.

In a Web article titled "Peace Building and Conflict Transformation," several essential ingredients of peace building and conflict transformation were explained that it should aim at channeling the energy generated by conflict in constructive, non-violent, rather than destructive and violent directions.

Conflict transformation accordingly occurs when violence ceases and/or is expressed in non-violent ways by normal socio-political processes in cooperating wider cross section of political decision makers, citizens, aid and development agencies, religious organizations, and social movements.

Conflict transformation may also require some kind of crisis management methods such as: conciliation, mediation, negotiation, arbitration, and collaborative problem solving processes which involve reconstruction and reconciliation.

Lederach, in his contribution on conflict transformation (1995), emphasizes the importance and place of peace, justice, truth, and mercy. He explains that just as justice and peace are often seen as being in opposition to each other, so are justice and mercy. Justice, he claims, involves "the pursuit of restoration, of rectifying wrongs, of creating right relationships based on equity and fairness. Pursuing justice involves advocacy for those harmed, for open acknowledgment of the wrongs committed, and for making things right. Mercy, on the other hand, involves compassion, forgiveness, and a new start. Mercy is oriented toward supporting persons who have committed injustices, encouraging them to change and move on."

Often it is assumed that one does one or the other, but not both. Justice, as it is often assumed, requires determining the truth and punishing the guilty party. Mercy, on the other hand, implies bringing forgiveness. Thus, if one prosecutes and punishes the guilty, mercy at best can involve leniency in the sentence. Punishment, however, seldom results in either reconciliation or restitution. Thus, the resulting "justice" is illusory.

The challenge, according to Lederach, is "to pursue justice in ways that respect people, and at the same time to achieve restoration of relationships based on recognizing and amending injustices." Thus, he argues that reconciliation involves the identification and acknowledgment of what happened (i.e., the truth), and an effort to right the wrongs that occurred (i.e., justice and forgiveness for the perpetrators--mercy). The end result is not only reconciliation, but--through true change--peace.

Those who come from a Pacifist background would emphasize that we learn from history that the violence that liberates can quickly become the violence that enslaves. As expressed by Brown (1986), when a new order of justice is created by murdering all who supported injustice, has injustice not merely changed hands? The way which is ultimately more revolutionary than violence is to repudiate the violent methods of one's opponents. Pacifists who have demonstrated this most effectively include the martyrs who sealed the witness with their blood.

There is need for witnessing together for justice and peace. Whatever our moods, God calls us to preach Christ crucified. Although a stumbling block and foolishness to many, the cross is the power and the wisdom of God. Whether or not all agree, there are responses and interpretations we can share (Brown, 1986).

We must learn to engage in the ministry of listening. We must be willing to welcome the opportunity to bear one another's burdens, therefore fulfilling the laws of Christ. In Nigeria there are millions of people who are hurting, many because of the recent violence created by Boko Haram, many of them suffering simply because much in society is organized to the advantage of others.

We need to be made aware of the oppressive structures hiding under the umbrella of religion, tribe, state, national and local government, and even education. We should be able to offer a compassionate and responsive ear to people who want to tell us their story of their suffering, persecution and oppression, whether they are Christian, Moslem, or of traditional religions. In this way we

can transcend our religious, tribal, or even racist tendencies through fellowship, respect and dialogue. Finally, we must join hands to support voices that challenge vigorously movements for justice which are non-violent and which build tolerance, respect, and trust.

Through the long era of human history, religion has been a major contributor to wars, bloodshed, persecution, hatred, and intolerance. Yet religion has also developed laws and ideas that have provided civilizations with a cultural commitment to critical peace-related values. The latter include empathy, an openness to and even love for strangers, an emphasis on human rights, unilateral gestures of forgiveness and humility, suppression of unbridled ego and acquisitiveness, interpersonal repentance and acceptance of responsibility for past errors as a means of reconciliation, and the drive for social justice (Gopin, 2000).

As we struggle and pray for conflicts to be resolved--in the home, in the community, in the nation and the world--there is a need for us to understand how religion can be used to resolve rather than exacerbate social and political conflicts in our environment. We need, as a matter of priority and urgency, to use a holistic approach to teach all adherents to the two major religions in Nigeria to help build and maintain a good balance of acceptability and tolerance for the good of all.

As we progress through the 21st century, the challenges presented by religious violence are ever increasing. This is indeed a time of testing for Christians and Moslems alike, a time when the skills of conflict resolution/transformation are needed more than ever to protect and strengthen our society.

CHAPTER FIVE

Corruption: The Christian Perspective

While religious persecution and violence have "taken center stage" in Northern Nigeria in recent times, other dangers threaten the very fabric of Nigerian society. In particular, one of them, corruption in government at all levels, requires our attention. This is an issue of long-standing and urgent concern to every upright citizen.

Nigerians, who are a very religious people, are groping in darkness, searching for God-fearing, faithful, honest, trustworthy, humane, reliable, fearless, firm, morally upright and incorruptible leaders--people who are responsible and of exemplary character and conduct.

It has come to a point in this country that when people hear the word "corruption," it seems as though it is something that has affected almost every citizen regardless of his religious practice. This is because corruption of various kinds has eaten deeply into the Nigerian system like a cancer. Defined as a decay and rottenness, a change for the worse, depravity and wickedness, corruption always is characterized by a loss of integrity and purity.

How frequently, for decades, we have witnessed this in our highest government leaders as successive civilian and military governments have taken power from their predecessors! Each government coming to power has included the fault of corruption to blame for the shortcomings of their predecessors. Yet almost all of the governments have suffered from what I refer to as A.I.D.S. (Acute Integrity Deficiency Syndrome).

Too many leaders, spiritual and temporal, throughout the country, speak the language of love, integrity, respect and discipline, but they live lives of corruption clothed in materialism, dishonesty, hypocrisy, lust for power, greed, and sycophancy.

As corruption in its many guises becomes the currency of social exchange, millions of our people are unsettled within themselves because their confidence in the values of their leaders, who are seen as the pillars of society, is badly shaken. All Nigerians, including the leaders themselves, know that we are suffering from the corrosive impact of corruption which threatens to affect and paralyze every sector. There is no doubt that if a nation is to survive and become a leader among nations, its spiritual and moral compass must be in good working order.

Increasingly one sees evidence that Nigeria, as Mason (1982) expressed, has arrived at a crossroads but has temporarily lost sight of the signposts. As long as the fabric of the nation is threatened because of corruption, the signposts will remain in obscurity and the small people of the nation--in particular the voiceless masses--will remain aliens under their own sub-Saharan sun.

One cannot mention the word corruption without thinking about ethics or morality. According to Lewis (1981), morality is concerned with three things: first, with fair play and harmony among individuals. Secondly, with what might be called tidying up or creating harmony within each individual. Finally, with the general purpose of human life as a whole--what man was made for, what course the entire fleet should be on, and what tune the conductor of the band wants to play.

Corruption does not bring fair play and harmony among individuals and it does not allow for harmony to develop within. Rather, it encourages lies, shoddy work, and hypocrisy--acting what one is not, claiming what one is not, and trying to demonstrate what one is not. The conduct of our leaders has, times without number, brought shame to our nation. Monguno (1988) refers to the behavior of our elders who are supposed to be mature, experienced, educated, enlightened members of the elite, and who are ironically called the cream of society in the national arena. In seeing this behavior, one has to admit that our system has been irrelevant and fails to serve its intended purpose.

How and why, he asks, did we churn out so many "fake" leaders in politics, public service, the judiciary, the armed forces, business, academics, labor--and even religious organizations--leaders who display shamelessly gross indulgence in corruption? In all levels of society these leaders have shown dishonesty, hypocrisy, moral degeneration, sycophancy, inordinate ambition, insatiable lust for power, nepotism, and above all, total lack of patriotism.

When we examine this subject from the Christian perspective, we cannot fall into the error of those who profess an allegiance to Christianity but then take a wholly unchristian attitude toward most of the population of the country. The Christian faith does not permit compromise on such issues. If we are to love the Lord our God with all our heart, soul, strength and mind, there is no room for conflicting allegiances. If we are to love our neighbors as ourselves, we cannot fail in a single instance to serve their true best interests in every available way. Corruption and bribery cause injury to our neighbor and destroy our vertical relationship with God.

Christian influence must affect Nigeria's politics, economics, and social concerns. Christian influence should be felt only when it comes from Christ Himself, through wholly willing servants whose convictions are rooted in understanding of the full gospel with its inescapable requirement that our society be progressively transformed into one of genuine brotherhood.

From the Christian perspective, the responsibility of every Nigerian is a serious one indeed. This is not because most Nigerians are dishonest or because a person has to be corrupt to get ahead in life. It is because the Christian is constantly called upon to reconcile as best he can the imperative demands of Christ's commandments with the basic facts about one's actions--the fact that no one can have his own way entirely about anything or at all times. There is need for compromise at times, and sacrifice.

Christians in Nigeria have to do their best to stamp out corruption and find ways to express practically, through their conduct, their Christian concern for the welfare, strength, development, and freedom of all their neighbors. The greatest motivating force in all human life is self-sacrificing love.

There must be strong voices to urge clear and challenging action on corruption and other issues that are confronting Nigerian society, because the full impact of Christian influence will not be felt until Christians stop unnecessary compromising and looking the other way. A new spirit, a spirit of prayer, repentance and confession, a spirit of responsibility to the Word of Christ on the one hand, and to our fellow human beings on the other, is beginning to move in our nation through such groups as Nigeria Prays, Congress on Christian Ethics in Nigeria (COCEN) and Transparency in Nigeria. But the movement is not fast enough or sufficiently powerful. It will not accomplish much until individual, consecrated Christians, political leaders, military leaders, and good people in great numbers are willing to see that they are called by God and their consciences to the elimination of bribery and corruption.

One fact is clear from this perspective and that fact is the full influence of Christ. His message with all of its implications must be carried into every realm of life. We must try to live without fear; we must build for the future as if there were to be one, regardless of our worst forebodings. As Voorhis (1951) expressed, there are moral issues that face mankind today on which the Christian must take his stand and bear his witness. One of these issues is corruption. To fail to act, to turn our backs on these problems and the distress of our fellow man is to violate the second commandment--to love your neighbor as yourself.

Corruption is as old as man himself. Men, according to the Bible, have connived together to be corrupt. Genesis 6:11 states that

"The earth was corrupt in God's sight and was full of violence," and when the passage says "earth," that includes Nigeria. Again, in Psalms 14:1,3, the writer speaks of the fool who in his heart says there is no god--he is corrupt, his deeds are vile; there is no one who does good. All have turned aside.

The Bible does not spare those who indulge in corrupt practices because, according to scripture, these people do not know God. To the pure, all things are pure, but to those who are corrupted and do not believe, nothing is pure. Both minds and consciences are corrupted. They claim to know God, but by their actions they deny Him. They are detestable, disobedient, and unfit for doing anything good (Titus 1:15-16). Further, "Extortion turns a wise man into a fool, and a bribe corrupts the heart." (Ecc. 7:7)

The message is loud and clear: all Nigerians, regardless of their background, tribe or religion, must join hands to curb corruption, to push for enthronement of probity, accountability and transparency in every realm of society--business, the economy, politics, the military, police, education, even religion.

While corruption has many components, the largest issue therein is bribery. As mentioned previously, corruption from the biblical standpoint may be social, political, or in any area of life; thus, bribery is found in all arenas. Socially, the Bible speaks of corruption as not acceptable to God. When a person attempts to influence anyone--especially a public figure--to take a bribe for any reason, both people involved are corrupted.

And, one would ask, why is bribery necessary? God's divine power has provided us with everything we need for life and godliness through our knowledge of Him and His message, though Him who called us by His own glory and goodness (2 Peter 1:3). There is no need for dishonesty!

Again and again the Word of God instructs us on how to curb corruption in society. In Second Peter we are told that we must work hard to be good, but even that is not enough. We must also learn to know God better and study to discover what He would have us do. Next, we must learn to put aside our own desires so that we become godly and patient, gladly letting God have His way with us. The next step is for us to learn to know and enjoy other people, and to appreciate them; thus, our love for our fellow men will grow deeply; that love will drive out any need for bribery or dishonesty in any form.

Another way to curb corruption in society is to avoid associating with people who are dishonest. The Bible clearly tells us to take no part in the worthless pleasures of evil and darkness, but instead we should expose and rebuke them. We must avoid temptation. In Exodus 23:8 we are told, "Do not accept a bribe, for a bribe blinds those who see and twists the words of the righteous." If it is wrong to take that bribe because it blinds the minds of those who would otherwise be able to distinguish between right and wrong, then it is also wrong to offer that bribe (O'Donovan, 1996). We see clearly that to offer a bribe, even when it is not expected, is to put temptation before someone, and to forsake justice and to break the law.

Bribery promotes greed (Proverbs 15:27). The Word of God in First Timothy 6:9 teaches us, and human experience shows us, that greed destroys people. And that when people trust in money, they do not trust in God (1 Tim. 6:17). It is a common fact that people steal and kill because of greed. In fact, many murders and ritual killings happen every year because of the love of money and wealth of all kinds. When bribery promotes greed, greed in turn destroys both people and nations.

Our responsibilities, as we examine corruption from the Christian perspective, are several fold. We must be courageous enough to refuse to offer or to accept bribery at every level of our lives--which includes the home and within personal relationships. We must pray to change the hearts of any who are tempted by bribery. If all would pray and would refuse to practice bribery, that would change the culture of the country.

It may not be easy for a Christian to do this; he may have to endure suffering or persecution at the hands of misled or evil men and women, even from some of our leaders who are themselves entangled in this web of destruction. We must trust God in this fight, no matter what the insult. The Bible promises that God rewards those who faithfully serve Him; Jesus said, "My Father will honor those who serve me." (John 12:26) Again in Matthew 5:11-12, Jesus said, "Blessed are you when people insult you, persecute you, and falsely say all kinds of evil against you because of me. Rejoice and be glad, for great is your reward in heaven."

We must be aware that, no, not "everybody is doing it." We must be counted among the few who are not corrupt. Let us form accountability relationships with others. We must be transparent, and not build walls of isolation and cover-up. We must provide mechanisms of check-and-balance, and prevent abuse of position for privilege. Nigeria is in dire need of men and women of integrity, men and women who cannot be bought, whose word is their bond, who put character above wealth. Men and women who will make no compromise with wrong, who will be as honest in small things as in great ones.

We as committed Christians have the mandate to set an example for our families, our communities, our nation, so that all may see in us the path that leads away from corruption to the desired state of honesty, integrity, and justice for all.

CHAPTER SIX

The Role of Christians in Democratic Elections: Politics as a Christian Vocation

I plead with you for all that makes strong citizens. First, clear convictions, deep, careful, patient study of the government under which we live, until you not merely believe it is the best in the world, but why you believe. And then a clear conscience, as much ashamed of public as of private sin, as ready to hate and re-hate and vote down corruption in the state, in your own party as you would be in your own store or church; as ready to bring the one as the other to the judgment of the living God. And then, unselfishness. And earnest and exalted sense that you are for the Land and not alone the Land for you. . . The readiness to wake and watch and do a citizen's work, untiringly, counting it as base not to vote at an election, not to work against a bad official or for a good one, as it would have been to shirk a battle in the war. Such a strong citizenship let there be among us; such knightly doing of our duties on the fields of peace. (Phillips Brooks)

Brooks is speaking here of the fight on a physical battlefield in an actual war against oppression. For us, the "battlefield" is within our justice system, and our "fields of peace" shall be realized when honesty governs our land. But he speaks clearly and broadly about our responsibilities as citizens, in particular as they pertain to the political realm.

While examining the dangers of corruption in Nigerian society, we also considered ways in which Christians are called to stand against that cancer in our land. One very important responsibility of each adult citizen in the fight against corruption is the part he plays in the process of democratic elections. For the Christian, elections on every level offer many opportunities for ensuring that able, honest candidates are voted into office. Only when our elected officials are first and foremost exemplary citizens, can we hope to see our country prosper and take its place among the mature and productive nations of the world. Thus we ask: what really is the role of Christians in the electoral process in Nigeria?

The role of the Christian in democratic elections is one of the myriad challenges of the age confronting this generation in Nigeria. The work for us begins at home and ends only at the borders of this country. There are four key words within this topic, namely "role," "Christian," "democratic," and "elections."

"Role," simply explained, is a person's part in real life. For example, she played the role of housewife as her children were growing up, even though she had been trained as a nurse.

"Christian" is used in no narrow or formal sense. It implies more than someone who has accepted Jesus Christ as Lord and Savior, but a person who, regardless of what his particular church membership may or may not be, is so devoted to the principles and teachings of the Gospels that he seeks with all his strength and intelligence to pattern his life after them. There have been examples like the great Ghandi, who followed this very path in a way far better than most of us who profess to be Christian. Christians must come to a full realization of the duties or responsibilities which they cannot, in loyalty to their religious beliefs and to their country, neglect or avoid.

Where some in their time have failed in this responsibility, some of us in the present age, with greater wisdom, knowledge, and ability, may succeed. We can and we must succeed. When, in the days ahead, devoted Christians decide to enter upon political careers, they should not have to work alone. Responsibility rests upon all of us who are committed to Christ's work on earth. The third key word is "democratic," defined as of, belonging to, or supporting democracy--treating people of all classes in the same way, making sure all are represented and treated in accordance with the principles of equal rights for all. Ideally, at least, a democracy does observe the principles of equality. It accounts to each citizen one vote and one vote only. This explains what "election" means: a choosing or being chosen, especially by voting. If one is "elected," the implication is that there has been a choice.

Democracy provides that the decisions of a majority of its citizens shall determine its course of action; and the losers in an election may not, in a democracy, resort to violence or upset the results (Voorhis, 1951). Democracy, he further explains, establishes law before which all citizens stand equal and to which they may appeal for redress of grievances, not only against their fellow citizens, but against the government itself as well.

Thus, a democracy by definition must allow freedom of expression and belief, and must constantly subject itself to change and reform at the will of the people. Democratic ideals permit no outcast; every citizen belongs to its own group; it thus preserves the basic principle of human dignity. As further stressed by Voorhis, democracy and democracy alone, of all existing forms of human social organization, offers full opportunity for the growth and development of the minds and spirits of the people. This is true because for democracy to be strong and vital, the people must achieve at least three things.

First, the people must have the constitutional right to decide their course of action. Second, they must have the will to assume responsibility for deciding that course of action. And third, they must know the means and methods whereby they can effectively carry out that responsibility, not only in the political aspect of life, but in the social and economic as well.

Unless all three of these elements are present, the other one or two cannot hope for long to exist. It is a known fact that no constitutional democratic government can endure the failure of its people to take seriously and to exercise diligently their duty to actively control their government and to give thought to its course and policy. Nor can a democratic society keep its vitality and strength if the people participate in the decision-making process only upon election days. Democracy must exist on a day-to-day basis.

The roots of any true democracy must be stuck deep in the groupings of its people in their local neighborhoods. It is in these locations that people devise ways for fitting their lives and activities together so that their bread and butter may be gained, their children educated, their health protected and improved, and their spiritual life developed, edified and strengthened.

It is also true that no democracy can be stronger or more creative in its national capital than it is in the rural crossroads community. Virile democracy demands, therefore, a constant growth in mind and spirit of its people. Democracy ideally provides peace and safety within a framework of order, which is the will of the majority of its people. If no proposed democracy has yet carried out in practice all the principles and ideals herein described, that is not the fault of democratic institutions in themselves, but is rather because of the failure of its citizens to use those institutions as they should.

The Christian must learn and understand the processes of democracy which represent an attempt to make it possible for the individual to express freely his conscientious convictions, even in so interdependent a society as the one in which we now live. He may not always have his way ("his way" may not always be the will of the majority), but he lives under free political institutions.

The Christian should also know that the political process begins with the people, where they live and work and carry out their day to day activities. Christian duty, in this sense, can be as broad as all the worthwhile occupations of our citizenry. This country, a multi-ethnic and multi-religious nation, is filled with men and women who do their work in the light of a Christian conscience and build the nation as teachers, farmers, doctors, architects, lawyers, miners, etc. But because of the way the political process works, it is not possible for such a population to do their Christian duty at election time unless Christian issues have been carefully drawn and presented to that population by Christian leaders for decision.

As pointed out by Voorhis (1951), it is equally impossible for one's Christian duty to be done at election time unless there are avenues that develop Christian candidates to serve. But again, there will be neither Christian issues clearly presented nor Christian candidates with any hope of election unless there are millions of devoted Christian men and women all over the nation performing from day to day the hard and oft times thankless routine tasks which constitute democratic political activity, Voorhis further stresses.

What does it take to win an election? An election is the action of choosing by vote one or more of the candidates of your choice for a position, especially a political office. And so, to win an election, it is necessary that more votes be secured for one candidate than for his opponents. The role of the Christian, therefore, is to familiarize more people with his candidate's name or to cause more people to like his candidate personally or to bring more people to agree with his candidate's ideas or ideologies than can be done for the opponent. This sounds simple, but it is not. In democratic elections, every adult citizen has the right to vote. But unfortunately not all do so, nor do all of those who do vote have a clear idea exactly what the issues are. Still others do not know exactly why they are voting as they do.

This is why labels of party, and, to a lesser degree, party organizations, are important factors in the outcome of elections. It is the responsibility of the Christian to help people cast more votes based on thought and conviction rather than as a result of habit or emotion. It is very important for the issues to be drawn as sharply as possible between parties and candidates in each election.

Thus, one of the most important services of elections is to force the real issues out into the open and to compel their honest, sincere and frank discussion. It is the responsibility of the Christian Church in Nigeria to be thoroughly awake to its full accountability for the fate of democracy and the nation.

There is, certainly, the need for practicing Christians, men and women who dare to apply the Great Commandments of our Lord to the practical problems of life, to seek through political activity to guide the course of their communities and their nation toward Christian objectives. We can no longer afford to isolate ourselves from the normal operations of the political system of our great country. The job of correcting what is wrong with a political organization can only be done from within--never from the outside. We must be active participants in political issues. We cannot take orders that are in any way contrary to our Christian principles. The Christian must work with the party of his choice in legitimate and proper ways.

The Christian candidate must adapt the method of personal contacts of one kind or another by himself. As he does this, his goal is to win the election. It is important for him to establish at least one vocal, effective supporter in every neighborhood in his constituency.

Christian supporters of such candidates should work effectively in informal conversations between friends and acquaintances. A more certain method is the house-to-house canvass which is desirable if done by tactful, sincere and earnest people. We are grateful for the communication boom in Nigeria today which provides another way: by telephone and cell phone. This is generally effective, and can be used to reach a larger number of people and is especially useful in areas where the candidate has no neighborhood or precinct workers.

The use of telephone campaigns, as employed in developed countries, can be carried on in a whole city by a group of willing people. These conversations should be brief and respectful, should avoid argument, and should be concerned mainly with acquainting the person called with the name of the candidate, his views, and the fact that he is a good, honest, dependable man or woman. This is true whether the caller is the candidate himself or one of his supporters.

The newspaper, whether local or national, is an important factor advertising in winning elections; it offers an important opportunity for the candidate to state his position on issues; it presents his name and views to many readers. And distribution of bills and pamphlets to as many people as possible is another effective way of presenting a candidate to the public. Whatever the message, it should be simple, clear, honest and straightforward as it addresses the community.

Neighborhood meetings, large or small, are also important and effective, and provide a time for face-to-face discussion and questioning. Those who do not wish to attend public meetings would be more likely to join a small group in the home of a friend.

As we consider the importance of participation of all Christians in democratic elections, we are reminded of Jesus' statement that the meek shall inherit the earth. His followers must find their way and their mission in a world gone mad with irresponsible power and leadership. God has given man the responsibility to develop, to build, and create institutions and relationships which will be good and strong enough to restrain evil uses of power and to channel it to the benefit of mankind instead of for its destruction.

The Christian has been given such civil responsibility because it can be fulfilled only by a people who are guided, inspired, and sustained by the strength of the spirit of God Himself. His unflinching guidance and inspiration come only to those who are willing to apply the best and simplest principles to every phase of their lives, both private and public, on every level of government. These principles can be found only in the Gospel of Christ.

Christians cannot afford to avoid responsibilities in the sphere of life where so many vital decisions must be made today--in the political arena. The role of Christianity in society cannot be over emphasized. The democratic institutions in Nigeria whether we accept it or not, offer the best climate for Christianity to face the enormous challenges before us. Christians must take up the full burden of witness for their faith by approaching politics as a Christian vocation, starting in their local communities where Christian relationships can develop best and most deeply.

We look for leaders who are genuinely influential in organizations and institutions, particularly those who share our visions on issues. Whether we choose to be involved as candidates for political office or as part of the group who will support and elect those officials, the same standards apply: honesty, integrity, the willingness to study and be open to listening to both sides of the issues, the desire to take an active part in providing truly democratic elections in our nation.

The task of the Christian who enters politics is a hard one, not because "most politicians are dishonest," or because "one has to be dishonest to get ahead in politics," as some would think, but because the Christian is called upon constantly to reconcile as best he can the imperative demands on the Christian Commandments with the basic fact about democratic politics--the fact that no one can have his own way entirely about any issue.

The Christian in politics has to do the best he can to find ways of expressing practically, through public political action, his Christian concern for the welfare, strength, full development, and freedom of all his neighbors.

There is a Herculean task to be performed in our country in preserving the integrity of the people's thinking. As Voorhis (1951) states, "In every crossroads hamlet and on every city street corner and in every home and in every meeting there is a Christian duty to be fulfilled." It is the Christian's duty to carefully explore the issues, to tell the simple truth, to put one's fellow citizens on guard against falsehood from whatever source and however cleverly packaged. It is our duty to help our fellow citizens to see the real facts of life and the challenges to that life in Nigeria today, along with possible solutions--not through rose colored glasses--and to persuade them to make decisions on the basis of all the evidence which Christian thinking presents.

If these criteria are met, elections will be truly democratic, and our elected officials will lead the country to a new era of development and productivity.

CHAPTER SEVEN

Facing the Challenge of HIV/AIDS--
Prevention, Control, Counseling, Education

Among the various challenges facing 21st century Nigeria is the continuing threat of HIV/AIDS. Although progress has been made in the prevention, control and treatment of this dread condition, much remains to be done.

First identified in Nigeria in 1985, HIV/AIDS was reported at an international AIDS conference in 1986. In 1987, the Nigerian health sector established the National AIDS Advisory Committee, followed by the National Expert Advisory Committee on AIDS (NEACA).

The government was slow to respond to the growing crisis, and not until 1991 was the first attempt made to assess the situation. However, when Olusegun Obasanjo became President in 1999, HIV prevention, treatment and care became one of the primary concerns of the government. Since that time, programs have been established which supply antiretroviral treatment to adults and children. Progress was sporadic, with drug supplies and treatment centers limited, and by 2006 only ten percent of HIV-infected women and men were receiving therapy. As a result, 41 new AIDS treatment centers were opened in 2006, with numbers receiving the drugs rising from 81,000 in 2006 to 198,000 by the end of 2007, according to

In 2010, the National Action Committee on AIDS (NACA)

established the National Strategic Framework for treatment covering the years 2010-2015, which aimed to reach 80% of sexually active adults and 80% of most at-risk populations with counseling and testing. It also aims to ensure that 80% of eligible adults and 100% of eligible children will be receiving anti-viral therapy in 2015. Finally, it provides for improving access to quality care and support for at least half of people living with HIV within that time frame.

Although the above statistics show promise, worldwide, Nigeria has the second highest number of new infections reported each year, partly because of the relatively larger population as compared with other African nations. An estimate on the website www.avert.org/hiv-aids-Nigeria lists around 3,400,000 adult HIV cases, with an estimated 3.7% of the population living with HIV; the incidence is much higher in urban than in rural areas. Approximately 210,000 people died from AIDS in Nigeria in 2011.

The difficulty in diagnosing and treating these infections stems from the ways in which they are transmitted: through heterosexual sex because of lack of information about healthy sexual practice, lack of condom use, and high levels of sexually transmitted diseases. Transmission through use of contaminated blood transfusions is the second largest source of HIV infection. Other sources of infection come from the following routes of transmission: mother to child; female sex workers; men having sex with men; and injecting drug users.

Adding to the dilemma is the fact that in some regions of Nigeria, girls are married at young ages and thus have little knowledge about means of protection. (In general, twice as many girls as boys engage in sexual activity before the age of 15.) Other problems have included restrictions on promotion of condom use; lack of comprehensive sex education to young people; and lack of knowledge within the general population.

From the above, it is clear that many avenues of approach to control and prevention should be available. One of the most important of these is education, as much of the general public has a limited knowledge of HIV/AIDS. The virus (HIV) that causes AIDS is a tiny organism that is too small to be seen with an ordinary microscope. It takes only a limited number of these viruses to enter one's body for one to become infected and later develop the condition called AIDS (Acquired Immune Deficiency Syndrome). AIDS is not a disease caused by witchcraft or as punishment from God, or from bad water or mosquitoes. HIV (Human Immunodeficiency Virus) belongs to a group of viruses called retroviruses, which are found in humans and not in animals or insects. There are several types, or sub-types, of HIV, the most common in Africa being HIV1 which accounts for 97.5% of the infection in Nigeria. HIV2 accounts for 0.4%, and the remainder of infected people have both viruses.

If one is infected with any type of HIV, he will be at risk for developing AIDS, and for many, death will be certain, as the virus reduces the defense ability of the body's immune system, making it "deficient." It is this system's job to protect the body from all kinds of infections and invaders by destroying germs that enter the body. The white cells in our blood are on the first line of this defense, and HIV attacks these cells, leaving the body open to the invaders.

Once the general public is made aware of the scientific facts surrounding HIV/AIDS and the ways in which it is acquired, the next step in the process of education is that of ensuring an understanding of prevention. Avenues for this include media campaigns to raise awareness--radio, television, text messages on mobile phones, for example--encouraging consistent condom use and increasing knowledge and skills for condom negotiation in single men and women between the ages of 18 and 34. Programs in schools are aimed at reaching the younger children.

One important aspect in the war against HIV/AIDS is that of counseling, which is an ongoing dialogue and relationship between a client or patient with the aims of preventing transmission of HIV infection and providing psychological support to those already affected. In order to achieve those objectives, counseling seeks to help infected people make decisions about their lives, boost self-confidence, and improve family and community relationships and quality of life. This counseling also provides support to the families and loved ones of infected patients so that they in turn can provide encouragement and care for those with the infection.

The World Health Organization does not see HIV/AIDS counseling as a one-shot informal discussion between the counselor and the client. Rather, it is seen as an integral part of the overall health strategy, specifically designed to enable the infected persons to define for themselves the nature of the problems they face because of their infection, and to assist them to explore solutions for containing their precarious health status so that they can reduce the impact and severity of those problems, both to themselves and their families, friends, neighbors, and colleagues at the work place or in schools. Seen in this way, the counseling becomes a "handy means of mobilizing the psychological, social, and material resources of people with HIV infection or AIDS, and those of their close associates as well as health care workers and others concerned with their care and support." (WHO, 1988)

The World Health Organization has used two basic concepts in HIV/AIDS counseling: Primary and Secondary Prevention Counseling. The former is given to those usually designated as the major risk groups, who may be currently at risk of AIDS infection but are not yet known to be infected, such as prostitutes and their clients, those with many sex partners, intravenous drug users, and personnel in the armed forces or jobs that require long periods away from home and family.

For the primary prevention counseling of these risk groups to be effective, each group needs to be addressed in the language they understand, and even at that, some may require extra encouragement and support before they can feel sufficiently persuaded to act upon the information made available to them. This is especially true because much of the information and instruction touches on subjects of a very personal nature: avoidance of casual sex and multiple sex partners; adopting safe sex practices, particularly involving the use of condoms; resisting the urge to succumb to sexual experimentation or any practice which may result in the transmission of body fluids in risky situations; refusing to use needles and syringes used by another person, etc.

In addition to the health-oriented reasons for maintaining safe sex practices, there are compelling Biblical admonitions against taking part in sex outside of marriage. In Exodus 20:14 one of the great Commandments states, "Thou shalt not commit adultery." Sex outside of marriage frequently brings guilt, shame and sadness; it often involves one partner seemingly being "used," and not truly loved. Many sexual encounters result in unwanted pregnancies, creating untold problems for mother and child, as well as destroying future plans for marriage and family. All in all, the arguments for keeping sexual expression within marriage far outweigh those which stem from sexual freedom outside of marriage.

Secondary prevention counseling emphasizes not prevention, since the persons being counseled are likely already infected, so much as stressing the implications of the infection and the ways in which the crisis of re-infection can be avoided. The counseling teaches alternative ways of seeking sexual gratification to minimize the risk of infecting others and avoiding further complication by compromising the standard of their health status through acquiring additional infections.

In organizing secondary prevention counseling encounters, especially with infected pregnant women as clients, the major issue to be addressed is that of the possibility or option of terminating the pregnancy to avoid the risk of prenatal transmission of the virus. To succeed in this venture, as Nwoye (1994) pointed out, the counselor must give sufficient consideration to how the cultural, familial, religious and medical factors can affect such critical and difficult decisions.

The general information that is communicated to patients at this level of the counseling enterprise includes the following:

1. Getting infected with HIV does not automatically mean that one already has AIDS

2. One can be infected with no symptoms and can still pass the virus on to others.
3. Whether one infected with HIV will go on to develop a full AIDS condition is related to the type of life style he is living.
4. Those who avoid getting re-infected and who receive a nourishing diet can
5. stay in better physical health, especially when such a healthy lifestyle is supported with access to fresh air, adequate sleep and daily exercise.

The general information contained in this chapter is only that: general. HIV/AIDS is a simple, yet complex issue which impacts Nigerian society at every level. There is no single, easy answer. Because of its endemic existence, cutting across gender, age, location, and economic status, the attempts to devise programs to prevent, control and treat it must be aimed at all strata of society.

The need for public awareness is a top priority in the fight against HIV/AIDS. Only when society in general understands its threat and is fully dedicated to listening to and working with the medical, educational, and theological experts can we hope to see true progress toward its eradication. Many, many Nigerians are affected directly or indirectly with victims in their family, friends, or associates. HIV is not a respecter of persons--rich or poor, young or old, educated or illiterate. It can be contracted in a variety of ways because it is caused by a virus which cannot be seen and may be passed from a seemingly healthy person to an unsuspecting victim. Treatment is not readily available in many localities, and may not be effective, especially when diagnosis has been delayed.

In addition to the personal responsibility of the ordinary citizen, the Nigerian government, along with international involvement, must assume the responsibility of funding more health facilities with adequate personnel, equipment, and medication.

As we Nigerians face this challenge of the present century, we must take on 21st century thinking: put away embarrassment, superstition, ignorance, and indifference in looking at the reality of this scourge. We must be willing to discuss it openly, and to be aware of risks that may expose us or those we love to this dread infection. We must earn its methods of transmission and seek out avenues of assistance--clinics, hospitals, medical personnel--if we suspect we have been exposed. We must make sure that HIV education reaches each member of our families, our schools, our communities. We must take responsibility for protecting our health and the health of our nation.

HIV/AIDS can be an overwhelming and frightening fact of life in this century. Only an open, concerted effort--beginning with each of us--can make a difference in its future prevention, control, and, eventually, eradication.

CHAPTER EIGHT

Creating a Healthy Society: The Theological Response to HIV/AIDS

While the overall welfare of the Nigerian nation depends upon strong families, strong communities, and strong national leadership, the physical and psychological health of its people is at the core of the country's ability to meet all of the challenges of the 21st century. A population ravaged by sickness cannot function wholly or productively. In a physically compromised state, moral corruption and other evils may flourish, and growth is stunted or non-existent.

Thus, it is imperative that the general public understand one of the most significant threats to our nation, that of HIV/AIDS. Next to those involved in the medical and educational professions, the pastor/theologian holds the responsibility of leading the community in facing the challenge of preventing, controlling and treating this deadly infection.

How and why is much of this responsibility placed in the hands of the ministry? In linking theology with HIV/AIDS, we must look at the theology of creation. This is because human beings live within God's creation. In fact, everything that is most valuable in a theology of creation may be expressed in terms of relationships. There are relationships within the Trinity between God and creation, both its human and non-human aspects; among human beings; and between human beings and the natural world.

When God completed His creation, He also provided freedom and the risk of our choosing evil. That is to say that God does not compel us to have good relationships, but leaves us free to choose whatever relationships we desire. He does not manipulate us into obedience like puppets.

The second important truth theology reveals to us about God is His love, affection, compassion, mercy and care. Hence, we experience fellowship with Him and fellowship with one another. The theological response to HIV/Aids in this case is real fellowship, which is authentic; it is shared with HIV/AIDS patients in a way that is not superficial, surface chit-chat. It is a genuine, heart-to-heart, sometimes gut-level sharing. It is a kind of fellowship that occurs when people are honest about who they are and what is happening in their lives. They share their hurts, reveal their feelings, confess their failures, disclose their doubts and fears, acknowledge their weaknesses, and ask for help and prayer.

Christian theology should remove pretence, role-playing, politicking, and superficial politeness about the reality of HIV/AIDS within the church, the family, community and institutions. It is only when we become open about our lives that we experience real fellowship and are able to minister to the needs of others--as well as to receive aid from them for ourselves. The Bible tells us, "If we live in the light, as God is in the light, we can share fellowship with each other. . .if we say we have no sin, we are fooling ourselves." (1 John 1:7-8)

It is true that the world thinks intimacy occurs in the dark, but God says it happens in the light. Darkness is used to hide our hurts, faults, fears and failures. But in the light we bring these out into the open and admit who and what we really are. Of course, being authentic requires both courage and humility. It means facing the fear of exposure, rejection and hurt. Why should those suffering from this dreadful affliction--and the society, the Church, the family, or those who share fellowship with them--invite such risks when they open themselves in honesty?

Theology tells us that it is the only way to grow spiritually and to be emotionally healthy. In the Book of James 5:16a we read, "Make this your common practice: confess your sins to each other and pray for each other so that you can live together whole and healed." We grow only by taking risks, and the most difficult risk of all is to be honest with ourselves and with others.

Another way in which theology responds to the HIV/AIDS threat is in urging people to experience mutuality--the art of giving and receiving, the act of depending on each other. First Corinthians 12:25 advises us that the way God designed our bodies is a model for understanding our lives together as a church; every part dependent on every other part. Mutuality in this sense builds reciprocal relationships, shares responsibilities and helps each other. Paul said, "I want us to help each other with the faith we have. Your faith will help me, and my faith will help you." (Romans 1:12) The Bible commands mutual accountability, mutual encouragement, mutual serving, and mutual honoring (Romans 12:10). The New Testament commands us over fifty times to do different tasks to one another and each other; Romans 14:19 urges us to "make every effort to do what leads to peace and mutual edification."

Each of us is not responsible FOR everyone in the Body of Christ or for everyone suffering from HIV/AIDS, but we are responsible TO them, to do whatever we can to help as many as we can. The Bible makes it clear that in real fellowship people experience sympathy. Sympathy is not giving advice or offering quick, cosmetic help. It is, simply, entering and sharing the pain of others. Sympathy says,   "I understand what you are going through, and what you feel is neither strange nor crazy." Today some use the word "empathy," but the Biblical word is "sympathy." It admonishes us "as holy people. . .be sympathetic, kind, humble, gentle, and patient." (Col. 3:12) Theologically, sympathy meets two fundamental human needs: the Word to be understood and the need to have one's feelings validated. Every time we understand

and affirm the feelings of another we build fellowship and a good relationship.

Theology also responds to those suffering with HIV/AIDS through the experience of sharing mercy. The theology of fellowship is a place of grace, undeserved favor, where mistakes are not rubbed in but are rubbed out. This happens when mercy wins over justice. Our children, relatives, neighbors or church members who are victims should not attract bitterness or resentment from us; rather they should have our sympathy and mercy, developing, and building healthy, robust relationships that create an atmosphere wherein we get along with each other, treating each other with dignity and respect and honor. We are called to learn to restore broken relationships brought about by the HIV/AIDS pandemic. We are to have the attitude of a father meeting his son with love, with no conditions attached, just as the father in the Bible met his prodigal son.

People living with HIV/AIDS commonly experience feelings of guilt and shame. Theology admonishes us to be sensitive to their damaged self-esteem as well as to the negative feelings or perceptions that accompany a collapsed self-concept. We need to assure these victims that God loves them deeply and wants only the best for them. Through the mouth of Jeremiah (29:11) God has said, "For I know the plans I have for you. . .plans to give you hope and a future." Such Divine Love is communicated not only by means of verbal assurances, but also most powerfully by human messengers of love, who, with loving acts, represent Christ's love incarnate to these unfortunate victims. If people with HIV/AIDS can experience firsthand such love and acceptance because they are valued human beings, they can surely learn to enjoy the blessings of the abundant life which Jesus promises to them.

The HIV/AIDS pandemic raises different theological issues in the areas of creation, human nature, the nature of sin and death, the Christian hope for eternal life and the role of the Church as the Body of Christ. Furthermore, the reality of AIDS raises issues, such as human sexuality, vulnerability, and mortality, which stir and challenge us in a deeply personal way. Christians and the Church struggle with these theological and human issues, and they differ, sometimes sharply, in their response to some of the challenges created by this plague. It is imperative that we learn to face the issues together, rather than separately, and that we work as a team toward a common understanding of the fundamental questions--theological, anthropological, ecclesiological--which are involved.

We thank God because we live by hope, which holds our questions and doubts within the larger frame of God's love and final purpose for our lives and for all creation. As we remember the suffering servant in Isaiah, we are called to share in the sufferings of persons living with HIV/AIDS, opening ourselves in this encounter to our own vulnerability and morality. As Christians we must respond to this call--certainly one of the most pressing issues facing our nation in the 21st century.

CONCLUSION

When we consider the progress that has been made in every aspect of Nigerian society during the 20th century, we are grateful to Almighty God for His guidance and direction on behalf of this great nation. Now as we plan ahead to increasing progress in the 21st century, we must look to that same source of strength and direction.

The future looks promising, but only if we are willing to be aware of the problems looming ahead and to commit ourselves to being part of the solution. The Christian community in Nigeria has been founded upon the scripture of the Holy Bible; its teachings provide a framework for life and belief for each individual as well as for the family and the community.

The importance of the family unit in society cannot be overstated, for it is the cornerstone upon which a community depends. Strong, united, Biblically-oriented families are the key to a healthy, mature, growing society. Children, who are reared in a loving household where the teachings of the Bible are not only read but practiced, will grow up to be responsible citizens who will work to solve the nation's problems rather than to become part of them.

With the strength of the Christian society based upon the Bible and theological teachings, it is imperative that pastors are adequately prepared to lead. The family and the community depend upon their expertise for leadership, instruction, comfort, and moral guidance. The pastor--along with educators and medical personnel--is the bulwark of society.

But the importance of honest, dependable, consistent political leadership is of utmost importance, as well. Without integrity in government, from the top levels down to the least significant elected posts, society will not prosper. Each individual adult must take responsibility to fulfill his duty in studying the issues, supporting candidates with integrity and strength, voting in every election, and, when appropriate, entering the field of politics himself.

When corruption enters the political arena, Christians are duty bound to search it out and expose it. Bribery and all forms of greed and dishonesty are a plague which will destroy a government, whether it is on the national level or within the community. Again we see that the battle against corruption of any kind begins in the home, where children are taught the importance of truth and openness. Nigeria has experienced corruption in government throughout recent years, and now it is up to the present generation to establish leadership that will prevent further problems.

Especially in times of the threat of violence, a strong government, unencumbered by corruption and political bickering, is essential to meet any dangers. All leadership is paramount as Nigeria faces the challenges of the 21st century, the most pressing of which is religious violence in these current days. The dangers of militant groups such as Boko Haram and ISIS are growing, threatening homes, churches, communities, and the nation itself. Because of the pacifist background of EYN the response to such violence must be one of peaceful conflict resolution. For the pacifist Christian, the situation is precarious. But meeting violence with violence cannot be the answer. Christ admonishes His followers to love their enemies, to pray for them. In 21st century Nigeria, where lives and property have been destroyed, this path may seem difficult to consider, but the Way of Jesus Christ has never promised to be easy. Whether faced in the home or the street or anywhere within the nation, violence calls for conflict resolution and/or transformation through dialogue, prayer, and mediation.

While threats from without may endanger our nation in the 21st century, threats from within must be addressed as well. One of the most serious continuing challenges is that of HIV/AIDS. Although great strides have been made in the treatment and containment of this malady, much work remains to be done. Education, awareness, funding for clinics, equipment, and medications, training of medical personnel--all must be addressed

In considering the plight of its victims, the issue of pastoral counseling is paramount, not only for the ill, but for the family, friends and all those with whom he may have been in contact. Only when the victims feel understood and truly cared about rather than ostracized, can there be real progress in both care and containment. HIV/AIDS touches many families in Nigeria without regard to gender, religion, age or location. Thus, its eradication must be approached on a holistic and national--as well as community and individual--level.

Nigeria faces a bright future. Challenges to that future abound, but when we are united in purpose, marching under the banner of Christ and with the Bible as our guide, no task will be too great. Our prayers for guidance will not go unanswered as our beloved nation takes its place in the 21st century.

REFERENCES

AIDS prevention and control: Invited presentations and papers from the World Summit of Ministers of Health on Programmes for AIDS Prevention. (1988). Geneva: World Health Organization ;

Baker, K., & Ward, H. (1990). Aids, Sex and Family Planning: A Christian View. Achimota, Ghana: African Press

Balswick, J., & Morland, J. (1990). Social problems: A Christian understanding and response. Grand Rapids, Mich.: Baker Book House.

Beacon of Hope Survey of TEKAN Churches, (2001) July/August, Unpublished, Jos

Bhatia, K., & Bhatia, B. (1974). The philosophical and sociological foundations of education, with a chapter on the educational philosophy of Marshall McLuhan. Delhi: Doaba House.

Bicket, Z. (1973). The effective pastor. Springfield, Mo.: Gospel Pub. House.

Blaikie, W. (1896). For the work of the ministry a manual of homiletical and pastoral theology (6th and rev. ed.). London: J. Nisbet

Bowers, P. (1989). More light on theological education in Africa. Journal of Evangelical Theology, iii(2), 11-18.

Bridges, C. (1967). The Christian ministry: With an inquiry into the causes of its inefficiency (From the sixth London ed.).

Brown, D. (1986). Biblical pacifism: A peace church perspective. Elgin, Ill.: Brethren Press.

Burkert, W. (1983). Homo Necons: The Anthropology of Ancient Greek Sacrificial Ritual and Myth. Berkley: University of California Press.

Calvin, J. (1962). Institutes of the Christian religion. Grand Rapids, Michigan: Eerdmans.

Calvin, J. (1962). Institutes of the christian religion. Grand Rapids, Michigan: Eerdmans.

Camara, D. (1983). Christ is Our Peace: Biblical Foundation for PeaceMaking. Reformed Church Press.

Carballo, M. (1988), The critical role of counseling in HIV/AIDS prevention and control; introduction in WHO edited proceedings AIDS prevention and control. Oxford: Perganum press.

Chickering, A., & Gamson, Z. (n.d.). (1991). Seven principles for good practice in undergraduate education. Biochemical Education.

Criswell, W. (1980). Criswell's guidebook for pastors. Nashville, Tenn.: Broadman Press.

Dakum, P. (2002). HIV/AIDS Counseling. RURCON Holistic Christian Counseling Seminar Paper, Unpublished, Organised by TLM, Nigeria.

Diary of Religious Fracas: The News December 25, 2008

Dobson, J. (1970). Dare to discipline. Wheaton, Ill.: Tyndale House.

Donovan, W. (1996). Biblical Christianity in African perspective(2nd ed.). Carlisle, U.K.: Paternoster Press.

Elaigwu, J. (1993). The shadow of religion on Nigerian federalism: 1960-1993. Abuja, Nigeria: National Council on Intergovernmental Relations.

Federal Ministry of Health (2001), Department of Public Health, National AIDS/STDS Control Program Technical Report.

Fellowship of Christian Students (2003), Towards an AIDS free Generation- AIDS is Real and it's in our Church. Jos: Honey City Press.

Garland, C. (2003). AIDS is real and it's in our church: Information about AIDS in Nigeria, how to prevent HIV infection, and encouragement towards a Christian response to the AIDS epidemic. Bukuru, Plateau State, Nigeria: African Christian Textbooks.

Garland, C. (2003). Ten great reasons why you should say no to sex before marriage. Jos: Honey City Press.

George, J. (2005). The call to pastoral ministry: In How to Shepard Biblically. By MacArthur

Goetz, D. (1992). Is Pastors' Family Safe at Home. Leadership, 13(2).

Gofwen, R. (2004). Religious conflicts in northern Nigeria and nation building: The throes of two decades 1980-2000. Kaduna, Nigeria: Human Rights Monitor (HRM).

Gopin, M. (2000). Between Eden and Armageddon. The Future of World Religions, Violence, and Peacemaking. Oxford: University press.

Hafemann, S. (1988). Seminary subjectivity and the centrality of scripture: Reflections on the current crisis in evangelical theology. Journal of Evangelical Theology, 31(2).

Handern, W. (1968). A lay man's guide to protestant theology. New York: Macmillan.

Holy Bible: Today's New International Version. (2005). Colorado Springs, CO: International Bible Society.

Hornby, A., & Crowther, J. (1998). Oxford advanced learner's dictionary of current English (5th ed., special price ed.). Oxford, England: Oxford University Press.

James, Kyoko, Tokuno, and Wellman (2004). Is religious violence inevitable? Journal for the Scientific Study of Religion.

Johnstone, P. (1993). Operation world: A handbook for world intercession (5th Revised Ed ed.). Grand rapid: Zandervan

Kaseman, E. (1964). Ministry and community in the new testament, essays on new testament themes. Fortress, Philadelphia

Kelly, G. (1966). A brief introduction to personal constructs theory: In Dannister (ed), perspective in personal construct theory. London and New York: Academic press.

Kolawole, J. O (2007), Lecture Delivered at WAATI Nigeria Zonal National Conference held at the UMCA Theological College, Illorin from August 6-9.

Koopman, G., & Hoogerwerf, S. (1982). Christ is our peace: Biblical foundations for peacemaking. New York: Reformed Church Press.

Lederach, J. (1995). Preparing for peace: Conflict transformation across cultures. Syracuse, N.Y.: Syracuse University Press.

Lee, J. (2007). The ultimate topical bible guide: Bible basis;. Aurora productions AG.

Lewis, C., & Hooper, W. (1981). Mere Christianity: An anniversary edition of the three books, the case for Christianity, Christian behaviour, and Beyond personality. New York: Macmillan.

Ludzer, E. (1983). Still Called to the Ministry. Moody Monthly, 83(7).

MacArthur, J. (2005). Pastoral ministry: How to shepherd biblically. Nashville, Tenn.: Thomas Nelson.

Mambula, M. (1999). The making of a happy and a successful family. Jos: Challenge Press.

Mason, T. (1982). The Pluralist Society and Moral Education

Maxey, I. (1987). Ministerial ethics: That the ministry be not blamed : A guide to ministerial ethics and etiquette. Salem, Ohio: Schmul Pub.

McDowell, J., & Bellis, D. (1982). Evidence growth guide the uniqueness of the Bible. San Bernardino, Calif.: Here's Life.

Miller, D. (1988). Counseling of Persons with AIDS in WHO, edited proceedings AIDS: Prevention and Control. Oxford: Perganum press.

Monuguno, S. A (1988). Corruption- Why it Thrives. conference on corruption . Lecture Conducted from Federal Ministry of justice -Institute of Internal Affairs, Lagos.

Mounce, R. (1960). The essential nature of New Testament preaching. Grand Rapids: Eerdmans.

Murray, A. (1975). How to raise your children for Christ. Minneapolis: Bethany Fellowship.

National Agency for the Control of AIDS (NACA), 2012. Federal Republic of Nigeria Global AIDS Response Country Progress Report.

Ndu, A. B (2007), Lecture Delivered at the National Conference of the Nigerian Zone of the West African Associated Association of Theological Institute (WAATI) at UMCA Theological College, Illorin.

Nwoye, A. (1994). AIDS, counselling and nutritional therapy. Jos, Nigeria: Fab Education Books.

Oden, T. (1983). Pastoral theology: Essentials of ministry. San Francisco: Harper & Row.

Ozment, S. (1980). The age of reform (1250-1550): An intellectual and religious history of late medieval and Reformation Europe. New Haven: Yale University Press.

Packer, J. (1973). Knowing God. Downers Grove, Ill.: InterVarsity Press.

Peace Building And Conflict Transformation: http:llwwwmu.edu/
academic/pcs/elements.htm

Phillips, K. (2007). Discovering Truth: Bidiscovering truth: Bible
keys to happier living; Bible Keys to Happier Living;. Aurora
productions AG.

Pickering, H. (1972). Seven Marks of a Christian.

Shenk, D. (1994). God's call to mission. Scottdale, Pa.: Herald Press.

Smith, G. (1937). A manual Greek lexicon of the New Testament (3rd
ed.). Edinburgh: Clark.

Spurgeon, C. H (1980), Lecture to my Students (Reprint of 1875),
Baker: Grand Rapids.

Stearns, R. (2009). The hole in our Gospel. Nashville, Tenn.:
Thomas Nelson.

Sugden, H., & Wiersbe, W. (1973). When pastors wonder how.
Chicago: Moody Press.

Swindoll, C., & Swindoll, C. (1991). The strong family: Growing
wise in family life. Portland, Or.: Multnomah Press.

The living Bible: Paraphrased.(1972). Wheaton, IL: Tyndale House.

Thompson, F. (1990). The Thompson chain-reference Bible: New
International Version : Containing Thompson's original and
complete system of Bible study : A complete numerical system of
chain references, analyses of books, outline studies of characters,
and unique charts : With (2nd improved ed.). Indianapolis, Ind.:
B.B. Kirkbride Bible.

Unwin, J. (1984). To discipline; as quoted by Dobson;. Jos: Challenge publications.

Voorhis, J. (1951). The Christian in politics. New York: Association Press.

Wanak, L.C (2008), Theological Education and The Role of Teaching in 21st Century: A Look at the Asia Pacific Region;

Warfield, B. (1988). The idea of systematic theology; The Necessity of Systematic Theology, ed. John Jefferson Davis;. Washington dc: University press.

Warren, R. (2002). The purpose-driven life: What on earth am I here for? Grand Rapids, Mich.: Zondervan.

Webster, N. (1983). Webster's new twentieth century dictionary of the English language, unabridged: Based upon the broad foundations laid down by Noah Webster. (2nd ed.). New York, N.Y.: Simon and Schuster.

WEBSTER, N., & Guralnik, D. (1966). Webster's New World dictionary. Elementary edition. David B. Guralnik: Editor in chief. Pp. v. 19. 808: Macmillan.

Werner, D. (1997). Challenges and Major Tasks for Ecumenical Theological Education in the 21st Century. Comp. Reports of Oslo World Conference on Theological Education: J.S Pobee (ed), Towards Viable Theological Education Ecumenical Imperative Catalyst of Renewal: WCC

Wikipedia, the Free Encyclopedia, Conflict Resolution energy. wikipedia.org/wiki/conflict_resolution

Wikipedia, the Free Encyclopedia, Religious Violence energy. wikipedia.org/wiki/religious_violence

Wilkerson, D. (2009). The Power of the Lord's Presence: World challenge.

Wilkerson, D. (2009). The Secret To Strength In Perilous Times: World challenge.

World Council of Churches (2002): Facing AIDS, The Challenge, The Church Response, A Study Document:. (2002). Geneva: World Council of Churches.

Youngblood, R. (1988). Excellence & renewal in theological education. Exeter, England: Paternoster.

ABOUT THE AUTHOR

Musa Adziba Mambula is a gifted teacher, preacher, public speaker, administrator, and a guidance counselor. He served as the Dean School of Education at the Kashim Ibrahim college of Education Maiduguri for 16 years, Provost /President Theological College of Northern Nigeria (TCNN) Bukuru near Jos for six years, Chairman Kulp Bible College Board Kwarhi-Mubi for seven years, Financial Secretary EYN Ministers' Council for six years, and Financial Secretary Counseling Association of Nigeria for four years. He was elected to serve as the National Spiritual Advisor for the Church of the Brethren in Nigeria for six years. Musa has authored and co-authored many publications including seven books and over forty Journal articles and several book reviews. Professor Mambula has participated in seminars and workshops at national and international levels and also served the church and church related bodies in different capacities. He is a graduate of Bethany Theological Seminary, Oakbrook Illinois and National Louis University Evanston-Chicago, Haggai Institute Singapore. Musa holds a Ph.D. in Educational Foundation from the University of

Maiduguri Nigeria. He is a Fellow of the Cooperate Administration of Nigeria, member International Leadership -LANGHAM Partnership in Biblical Preaching, member International Association for the Promotion of Christian Higher Education, and served as a Fellow at the Anabaptist and Pietist research center in Elizabethtown College, a member of the Transparency International in Nigeria. He has received numerous awards including a Distinguished Leadership in Socioeconomic Development of Nigeria and for Promoting Excellence in Leadership through Integrity, Accountability, and Transparency. Musa and his wife Sarah "Digni"(sweeter than honey) have four children and four grandchildren. They presently live in York Pennsylvania.

Printed in the United States
By Bookmasters